VIEWS ON WOMANHOOD

Views on Womanhood

A Translation and Reading of Muṣṭafā Ṣabrī Efendī's (d. 1373/1954) "Qawlī fī 'l-Mar'a"

Translated by

Muzzammil al-Nadwī and Junayd Greer

MUNTAHĀ
LONDON | HOUSTON

ISBN–13: 979-8-9899114-1-7 (Paperback)

Library of Congress Control Number: 2024931265

Front cover image by Muntaha Press LLC
Book design by Muntaha Press LLC

Typeface for the Latin script: "Brill".
Licensed by: I Love Typography Ltd

Printed by Muntaha Press LLC
First printing edition 2024.

Muntaha Press LLC
254 Chapman Rd, Ste 208 #15883
Newark, Delaware 19702

www.muntahapress.com

DEDICATION

To the women of Gaza, who–at the time of this writing–sleep under constant bombardment in their veils, hoping that if they do not survive the night, their bodies will retain their dignity when pulled from the rubble. While this translation may not risk the bravery and resilience with which these women sacrifice their lives for the revival of Islam, we pray that it may help promote their cause–one of devout modesty, enduring spirit, and true emancipation in the servitude of Allāh.

CONTENTS

ACKNOWLEDGMENTS

We would like to thank our dear friends and colleagues *Mawlāna* Haroon Anis, Dr. Zeeshan Chaudri, and *Shaykh* Rashid Khan for their help in editing this book, along with their valuable suggestions in translating some of its more difficult passages.

In addition, we are grateful to *Shaykh* Muḥammad Wā'il al-Ḥanbalī who published *Qawlī fī 'l-Mar'a* again in 2019 with Dār al-Lubāb, reviving a lost gem of scholarship whose relevance is greater now than perhaps ever before. We used his edition of the text throughout the translation, using his separation of paragraphs, translating his beneficial footnotes, and dividing the work into sections according to his example. With the help of our close colleague and friend *Shaykh* Hafizur Rahman, a pupil of *Shaykh* Wā'il, we were able to contact him. Despite being ill at the time, *Shaykh* Wā'il was kind enough to provide us a foreword for this book and shower us with words of encouragement for the project.

We are also indebted to *Shaykh* Muḥammad Ṣāliḥ al-Ghursī, whom we had the pleasure of meeting at his madrasa in Konya, with our friend *Shaykh* Bilal Cooper. His support for this project, along with detailed insights into the life and scholarship of Muṣṭafā Ṣabrī, proved invaluable to this translation. *Shaykh* al-Ghursī emphasised how critically underappreciated Ṣabrī's works are today despite their urgent relevance; we hope this work can contribute to reviving interest in Ṣabrī's thought among a wider readership.

FOREWORD

مقدمة

بسم الله الرحمن الرحيم

الحمدُ لله رب العالمين، والصلاةُ والسلامُ على سيدنا محمد، وعلى آله وصحبه أجمعين.

أما بعدُ:

فلا تزال قضيةُ المرأةِ شُغلَ الغربِ وهدفَهم، يريدون من ورائها إفسادَ الأسرةِ المسلمة كما فسدتْ أسرتهم، ويرمون مِن خلالها إلى تفكيكِ المجتمع المسلم كما تفكّك مجتمعُهم، فانتهض لهذه المسألةِ العلامةُ المجاهد، وشيخُ الإسلام - زمنَ الدولة العثمانية - مصطفى صبري أفندي رحمه الله تعالى، وذلك في كتابِه العجاب: (قولي في المرأة)، وقد ألف هذا الكتابَ رغمَ آلامِ هجرتِه من تركيا، وعدمِ استقراره في البلاد التي رحل إليها.

وقد ذكَر في مقدمة كتابه: أنَّ مسألةَ المرأةِ كانت - فيما سبق - هي الفارقَ بينَ الشرقِ والغرب، وبينَ المسلمينَ وغيرِهم، ولم يكن يخطر بالبال أن يجدَ الغربُ في نسائه المكشوفةِ مقلِّدًا لهم مِن أبناء الشرق المسلم، المعروفِ بغَيرتِه على نسائه!

فألَّف هذا الكتابَ رادًّا على دعاةِ تكشُّف المرأةِ وسفورِها، وذكَر فيه حُججًا عقليةً ومنطقيةً، ورُدودًا اجتماعيةً وطِبِّية، ولم يردَّ عليهم من خلال النصوصِ الشرعية، التي لم تعدْ تلقى اهتمامًا عندَ أولئك المتحرِّرين!

وكذلك تكلم على مسألة التعدد بما يكفي ويشفي، وأنها من حلول الخالق الخبير، لهذا المخلوق الضعيف، ولا يخفى أن ذلك يكون بضوابط وتوجيهات شرعية واضحة

فأكرمني الله واعتنيتُ بالكتاب، وتتبّعتُ دعاةَ الانفتاح والتفلُّتِ وتحريرِ المرأة، الذين ظهروا بدايةَ القرنِ الماضي، وكان تتبُّعي لهم مِن خلال كُتبِهم، ومما نُشِر مؤخَّرًا من كتبِهم ومذكراتِهم أنفسِهم، فوجدتهم كانوا على ارتباطٍ وثيقٍ بالمحافلِ الماسونية، والأنديةِ والاجتماعات الأوربية، ونسأل الله السلامةَ والعافية

وبعدَ ذلك أقول: إنَّ مِن أعظمِ نِعم الله عليَّ أنَّ أُمي - حفظها الله - امرأةٌ محجبةٌ، وكذلك أُسرتي وأهلُ بيتي

ثم قام الأستاذان مزمل الندوي وجنيد جرير بترجمة هذا الكتابِ إلى اللغة الإنكليزية، وهذا فيه جهدٌ شاقٌّ بلا ريب؛ وذلك لقوة عبارة المؤلف ووجازتِها، سائلًا الله أن يُثيبَهما خيرَ الثواب، وأن يجعلَ هذه الترجمةَ سببًا في الدفاع عن دين الله، والذبِّ عن محارمِ الله.

وكتبه الفقير إليه تعالى
محمد وائل الحنبلي
عفي عنه
وذلك في مدينة عينتاب التركية، على أرض بلاد الشام المباركة
10 جمادى الآخرة 1445هـ
23 كانون الأول 2023م

In the name of Allāh, the Most Gracious, the Most Merciful

All praise is for Allāh, Lord of the Worlds; [we send] salutations and prayers upon our master Muḥammad, his family, and all his Companions.

As for what follows:

The issue of "the woman" remains the object of the West's preoccupation and constant efforts. They insidiously desire [through promoting this cause, however] the corruption of the Muslim family, just as their own families have been corrupted. They [seek to] use this as a vehicle to dismantle Muslim society, just as their own societies have been dismantled [by it].

The great scholar and fighter, *Shaykh al-Islām* of the Ottoman Empire, Muṣṭafā Ṣabrī Efendī rose [to challenge] this cause in his remarkable book "Views on Womanhood." He composed this work despite the pains of migration he carried from Türkiye, while not yet stable in his new refuge [in Egypt].

He mentioned in the introduction to his work that "the issue of women has from a time not far [from our own] been the greatest point of distinction between the East and the West, and between Islam and other religions in society. This difference is so great that one could hardly imagine the West would find anyone among the Eastern Muslims, who are known for their protective jealousy (*ghayra*), to follow them in the exposure of their women..."

He wrote this work in refutation of those promoting women's unveiling and exposure, mentioning therein logical and intellectual proofs against [them], as well as counter arguments from social and medical [perspectives]. He abstained from using textual proofs [from religious sources], as these would not hold much worth among those liberals.

He also spoke on the issue of polygamy in a comprehensive, sufficient manner, [mentioning] that it is a solution from the All-Knowing Creator for we weak created beings–while being applied, as all are aware, with divinely-highlighted clear directives and regulations.

Allāh honoured me, and I was able to work on the book. In pursuing the proponents of unveiling, freedom, and the emancipation of women–those who arose at the beginning of the last century–through perusing their works, as well as their own books and notes published later [in life], it became apparent to me that they held close ties with [various] masonic lodges, as well as European circles and societies. We seek safety and refuge from Allāh.

Finally, I must declare that it is from Allāh's greatest blessings and favours upon me that my mother–Allāh protect her–is a covering woman, as are [the women in] my family and those in my home.

Thereafter, the two *ustādhs*, Muzzammil al-Nadwī and Junayd Greer, undertook the task of translating this work into English, which must have no doubt been a strenuous endeavour, due to the strength of the author's composition, as well as its brevity. I pray that Allāh grants them the best rewards, and that He makes this translation a means of safeguarding the religion of Allāh, and a defense for that which it holds sacred.

Written by one who is destitute before the Almighty,

Muḥammad Wā'il al-Ḥanbalī,
May Allāh pardon him,
In Gaziantep, Türkiye–in the blessed lands of al-Shām,
10th Jumāda II, 1445 / 23rd December, 2023.

TRANSLATORS' PREFACE

Introduction

Traditionalists today are often the object of widespread criticism in popular Muslim culture. They face attacks from academic circles, compounded by crass insults from various segments of the Muslim population. Among the chief grievances raised, even by those sympathetic to their plight, is that traditionalist scholarship has failed to keep pace with the various moral, social, and political quandaries currently facing the *Umma*.

This is true to a minor extent. Certainly, some Indian *madāris* (sing. *madrasa*) for example did retreat from society at the dawn of modernity.[1] Some circles of scholarship did abandon their societies to solve the challenges of modern life themselves, trading the easy comfort of abstract scholasticism and renunciant solitude for the hard-won reward of active involvement in the world of generation and corruption. Seeing lay Muslims in turn abandon their counsel, like a self-fulfilling prophecy, the scholars' isolation was vindicated. *Madāris* were built far from major cities and the real prospect of their students ever playing a leading role in the lives of cities now alien to them grew ever distant.

The logic of markets and money saw young Muslim elites, who in a different age would have received a classical education, instead graduate from Western institutions–"English in taste, in opinions, in morals, and in intellect," as Macaulay put it.[2] The *madāris* would go on as homes for orphans and second sons, until some schools were compromised by the spread of strange ideas endowed with a worldly vigour then as foreign as their provenance.

Despite this, many other *madāris* were designed as centres of socio-political reform and activism. 19th-century Indian Ḥanafī scholars inherited the tradition of their Mughal forebears, establishing *madāris* as power bases from which to struggle against colonialism and the erasure of Islam from public life; among them Dār al-'Ulūm Deoband.

---

[1] For more, see: Moosa, Ebrahim. *What Is a Madrasa?* Edinburgh: Edinburgh University Press, 2015, 104–105.

[2] Macaulay, Thomas Babington. *Macaulay's Minute on Indian Education*. February 2, 1835. National Archives of India.

Founded in 1867 in the aftermath of the Indian Rebellion a decade prior, the Deobandi movement and its early thinkers were inspired in part by Sayyid Aḥmad (d. 1246/1831) and Shāh Ismā'īl's (d. 1246/1831) *jihād* against Ranjit Singh (d. 1839) in the Punjab that sought to "establish a legitimate Islamic political order on the Subcontinent." Deoband's founders Muḥammad Qāsim Nānotwī (d. 1297/1880) and Rashīd Aḥmad Gangohī (d. 1323/1905) were politically active against British colonialism. Nānotwī, in particular, envisioned the *madrasa* graduating pupils at an early age so they could supplement their religious training with further secular education, thereby equipping them with the tools necessary to actively engage in social reform.[3]

Succeeding generations of the Deoband movement have spawned major and varied efforts at the reform and revival of Muslim societies, from Hussain Ahmad Madni's (d. 1377/1957) Jamiat Ulama-i-Hind, which worked towards Indian independence, to Ashraf 'Alī Thanwī's (d. 1362/1943) pan-Islamic activism, agitation for the reinstatement of the Caliphate, and his students' creation of the influential Jamiat Ulema-e-Islam which provided the religious grounding for the foundation of Pakistan.

Even the Taliban movement which now leads Afghanistan traces its intellectual heritage within the Deobandi school. In fact, the movement is perhaps the most accurate depiction of what the early founding fathers of the seminary envisioned from their graduates. As Moosa asserts, "Even if some despise the Taliban's affiliation to Deobandism, it is nevertheless a version of Deobandi theology on steroids."[4]

In the colonial and post-colonial Arab world, amid political chaos, religious institutions found themselves grappling with foreign philosophies. Egypt's Al-Azhar University continued to produce 'orthodox' scholars, only for them to share company and lecterns with heterodox reformists clothed in religious garb. The schizophrenic character of Egyptian Islamic scholarship persists today.

From the rationalist reform of Sir Sayyid Aḥmad Khān (d. 1306/1898) and the Aligarh Muslim University in India, to the Salafist reform of Jamāl al-Dīn al-Afghānī (d. 1315/1897), Muḥammad 'Abduh (d. 1323/1905), and Rashīd Riḍā (d. 1354/1935) in Egypt, or the more isolationist approaches of various strains of Wahhābī thought in the Najd region of Arabia, many

---

[3] Manāzir Aḥsan Gīlānī, *Sawāniḥ-e Qāsmī*. Dār al-'Ulūm Deoband, 1975, 2/280-285.

[4] Moosa, Ebrahim. *What Is a Madrasa?* Edinburgh: Edinburgh University Press, 2015, 105.

modern Muslim movements appear to fall under one of two categories as regards their response to the modern world; acquiescence or retreat. We must look beyond.[5]

Should it be conceded that the Islamic tradition represents a worldview and way of life fit only to exist isolated at the margins of contemporary civilisation, surrendering all practical claim on universal moral authority, then it rightly should have no substantial involvement in the life of modern societies. Should it be conceded that the Islamic tradition has been misconstrued, and in actual fact agrees sycophantically with modern liberal thought in all questions of real importance, then people can hardly be blamed for favouring the original source over an imperfect copy, and abandoning the faith altogether. To admit either conclusion would be to undermine the belief that Islam is a vital force able to accommodate and meaningfully guide human beings across cultures and times.[6]

The truth is that many scholars did carry the authentic tradition through this difficult period. They did not surrender the faith to modernity, nor did they flee from it. Rather, they undertook the challenge of grappling with modern ideas on their own merit, and exposing their feeble foundations.

Scholars such as the Tunisian polymath Ibn ʿĀshūr (d. 1393/1973) would convincingly promote Islamic pedagogy over its modern replacements in *Alaysa 'l-Ṣubḥu bi Qarīb*. Abū 'l-Ḥasan al-Nadwī (d. 1420/1999), a scholar and historian from India, would strive in *Mādhā Khasira 'l-ʿĀlam bi Inḥiṭāṭ al-Muslimīn* to combat the encroachment of historical revisionism on the central place of Islamic civilisation in world history. Yet perhaps the most erudite voice lost in the noise of the 20th century is the last *Şeyhülislam* of the Ottoman Empire, Muṣṭafā Ṣabrī Efendī.

---

[5] For further discussion of the modernist–traditionalist divide, see: Muhammad Qasim Zaman, *Islam in Pakistan*. Princeton University Press, 2020, 9–10.

[6] The well-known Islamic modernist thinker Fazlur Rahman offers an insightful perspective on this problem, arguing that the narrow-minded social outlook of some *ʿulamāʾ* is itself conducive to the emergence of secularism. In a 1966 article he writes, "Although almost all sections of the Muslim society are agreed in accepting at least the economically developmental forms of modernity and at the same time to preserve Islam, it has been difficult for them to devise a method whereby both are meaningfully integrated. So far as the 'Ulama' are concerned, although they accept the technological benefits of modern life, they are not only not willing to accept the consequences of modern education but are even by and large quite unaware of these consequences and think that both the traditional beliefs of Islam, as they were formulated by mediaeval theologians, and the traditional law can be kept completely intact and immune from modern influences. They would, for instance, while welcoming modern industry, still think that the giving and taking of interest can be strictly forbidden. It is this attitude of the 'Ulama' which is directly responsible for secularism in the Muslim world." See: Rahman, Fazlur. "The Impact of Modernity on Islam." *Islamic Studies* 5, no. 2 (1966): 119.

In his magnum opus, *Mawqif al-'Aql wa 'l-'Ilm wa 'l-'Ālam*, Ṣabrī counters Enlightenment thinkers and their modernist successors in metaphysics, epistemology, theology, and more. He also defends the institution of the Islamic Caliphate against its modernist detractors in *al-Nakīr 'alā Munkirī 'l-Ni'ma min al-Dīn wa 'l-Khilāfat wa 'l-Ummah*. His work *Mawqif al-Bashar taḥta Sulṭān al-Qadar* defends traditional Ash'arī doctrine on predestination in response to claims that this belief was primarily responsible for the underdevelopment of Muslims as a civilisation in comparison to the West.[7] He uncompromisingly defends the centrality of the Arabic language in Islam in *Mas'alat Tarjamat al-Qur'ān*, a work written in response to the Kemalist removal of Arabic from Turkish daily life and religious practice.

Qawlī fī 'l-Mar'a, translated here for the first time, is Ṣabrī's perspective on the modern corruption of authentic Islamic womanhood. Here, he responds to feminist activists of the early 20th century, defending the wisdom in polygamy, Islamic gender segregation, the veil and modest dress.

Across his works, Ṣabrī makes a point of addressing misguided beliefs as articulated by their foremost representatives, and in their own words. While in *Mawqif al-'Aql*–a critique of Enlightenment philosophy–Ṣabrī cites Bacon, Darwin and Kant, in other works addressing Islamic modernism, he challenges Jamāl al-Dīn al-Afghānī, Muḥammad 'Abduh, Muḥammad Muṣṭafā al-Marāghī (d. 1364/1945) and Maḥmūd Shaltūt (d. 1383/1963).

In *Qawlī*, the shaykh makes a specific effort to counter the Muslim feminists of his time, such as Sa'd Zaghlūl (d. 1927), Hudā Sha'rāwī (d. 1947), Qāsim Amīn (d. 1908), and Aḥmad al-Ṣāwī (d. 1989), and quotes from them at length. Such people are all the more dangerous than the Europeans who inspire them, says Ṣabrī, because their familiarity with Islamic society makes them more effective in promoting their agenda.[8]

Although Ṣabrī lived a life in politics, he never allowed worldly expediency to complicate his dedication to upholding the truth. None, not

---

[7] Ṣabrī's views in the work relating to determinism and free will were heavily criticised by his contemporary Muḥammad Zāhid al-Kawtharī, who held the traditional Māturīdī positions on both, in his "*al-Istibṣār fī 'l-Taḥadduth 'an al-Jabr wa 'l-Ikhtiyār*." While both identified with the Ḥanafī school in a legal capacity, Ṣabrī often inclined to the Ash'arī school in various creedal points, while al-Kawtharī held staunchly Māturīdī positions, more typically associated with Ḥanafism.

[8] Ṣabrī, Muṣṭafā. *Qawlī fī al-Mar'a wa Muqāranatuhu bi Aqwāl Muqallidat al-Gharb*. Beirut, Lebanon: Dār Ibn Ḥazm, 1935, 59.

even arch-conservatives sympathetic to his views were immune from Ṣabrī's criticism when he felt that they too strayed into modernist error. The otherwise conservative Egyptian shaykh Muḥammad Bakhīt al-Muṭīʿī (d. 1354/1935) is reprimanded in *Mawqif al-Bashar* for his concessions on predestination (*qadar*)–a hallmark of the Ashʿarī school–in deference to the modernist claim that this fatalistic outlook was a cause for Muslims' scientific backwardness.[9] Ṣabrī writes:

> "Shaykh Bakhīt did not cure an old disease by removing the obscurity covering the root of the issue. Nor did he cure the new disease by dispelling censure of the doctrine of predestination, and rejecting the claim that this is the reason for the Muslims' inability to keep pace [with modernity]. Rather, he spoke in a manner that seemed to capitulate towards those spreading such rumours and focused on devotedly reiterating one's abstention from the doctrine of [divine] compulsion (*al-jabr*), even if that may lead to rejecting predestination."[10]

Though often overlooked, Ṣabrī's legacy endures. His influence persists through students and associates such as Muḥammad Zāhid al-Kawtharī (d. 1371/1952) and ʿAbd al-Fattāḥ Abū Ghudda (d. 1417/1997), who often spoke of their debt to Ṣabrī and echoed his words to pupils wrestling with modern concerns. His works, whether in Arabic or Turkish, have remained in print and in the minds of Muslims since his death. His student Abū Ghudda, one of the main ḥadīth scholars of modern times, called *Mawqif al-ʿAql* "the book of the century."[11]

Ṣabrī's works were insightful and relevant in his own time, and remain so today. Many of his observations on the problems inherent in 'modern' gender norms in *Qawlī* could as easily describe the world today as a century prior. On that note, studying Ṣabrī's works and translating them to English for a new readership becomes imperative to carry on his mission addressing the crises of the modern world, which have only grown more extreme since Ṣabrī's time. We offer this translation as a modest step in that direction.

---

[9] For a detailed study on Bakhīt al-Muṭīʿī's complex point of view on modern issues, see: Quadri, Junaid. *Transformations of Tradition: Islamic Law in Colonial Modernity*. Oxford, England: Oxford University Press, 2021.

[10] Ṣabrī, Muṣṭafā. *Mawqif al-Bashar taḥta Sulṭān al-Qadar*. Cairo, Egypt: al-Maṭbaʿa 'l-Salafiyya, 1933, 22.

[11] Gharad, Amin. "A Torch in the Ottoman Twilight: The Life and Struggles of Şeyhülislam Mustafa Sabri Efendi (1286–1374/1869–1954)." *Journal of Hanafi Studies* 1, no. 1 (2022): 141.

The Life of Muṣṭafā Ṣabrī

Muṣṭafā Ṣabrī was born in Tokat, modern-day Turkey, hence the toponymic 'al-Tūqādī' ('the one from Tokat') attached to his name. His father, Ahmet b. Mehmet Kazabadi, and Ṣabrī's mother were both of noble Turkish heritage. He notes that "I was born in the heart of Anatolia in the city of Tokat. My parents, their parents, and the successive generations before were all Anatolians of noble Turkish heritage."[12]

He was born on the 12th Rabī 'l-Awwal 1286 AH, corresponding to the 21st of June, 1869 AD. He was raised in a religious, scholarly household. He memorised the Qur'ān by the age of 10 under the tutelage of numerous scholars, including Ahmet Efendi Zülbeyzade (d. 1322/1904). His father was a righteous man committed to establishing his son as a scholar of the religion. He would regularly invite scholars and teachers to his home in order to foster an environment of education and erudition for his son Muṣṭafā.

After completely memorising the Qur'ān, Ṣabrī travelled to Kayseri to further his studies. During the Ottoman period, the city was a centre of Islamic learning and on par with places such as Konya and Istanbul in the religious sciences. Ṣabrī spent his time here studying logic and theology with the Central Asian scholar Muḥammad Amīn al-Dūrīkī.

After his time in Kayseri, he set out for Istanbul where he would complete his traditional education under the tutelage of Ahmet Asım Efendi Gümülcineli (d. 1324/1906), a scholar from Gümülcine in present-day northeastern Greece. Ṣabrī's teachers in Istanbul, like himself, hailed from the provinces and graduated to teaching at the *madāris* of the capital, as was the typical career path for late Ottoman *'ulamā'*.[13] Gümülcineli was so impressed with Ṣabrī's talent in the Islamic sciences that he married him to his own daughter. By this stage of his studies, he was just 22 years-old.

His marriage to Gümülcineli's daughter, Ulviye Hanım, gave him three children, one boy and two girls. His oldest, İbrahim, would take after his father, accompanying him in his travels and intellectual efforts against secular thought. In later life, Ibrāhīm Ṣabrī worked as a university professor in Benghazi, Libya, and then Alexandria University in Egypt. Ṣabrī's next

---

[12] Ḥilmī, Muṣṭafā. *al-Asrār al-Khafiyya warā'a Ilghā' al-Khilāfa al-'Uthmāniyya*. Beirut, Lebanon: Dār al-Kutub al-'Ilmiyya, 2004, 98.

[13] Bein, Amit. "'Ulama and Political Activism in the Late Ottoman Empire: The Political Career of Şeyhülislâm Mustafa Sabri Efendi (1869–1954)." In *Guardians of Faith in Modern Times: 'Ulama' in the Middle East*, 105:69. Social, Economic and Political Studies of the Middle East and Asia. Leiden, The Netherlands: Brill, 2009.

child, Sabiha, married the famous 20th century Egyptian calligrapher, Muḥammad 'Alī. His final daughter, Nazahat, passed away in Istanbul in 1986.

Intellectual Activities

After completing his studies under Shaykh Asım Efendi in Istanbul, Ṣabrī passed the general examination for Ottoman scholars in 1890, allowing him to teach. He began at the Mehmet Sultan Fatih Mosque where his pupils included the likes of Said Efendi and the Palestinian Kāmil Mīrāth (d. 1376/1957) who went on to become prominent scholars in their own right. After years of teaching there, in 1896 he was granted the position of Imām and teacher at Asariye Mosque in the Beşiktaş district. He was then appointed as a teacher of Qur'ānic exegesis (*tafsīr*) at Vaizin Medrese, and selected by the Council of Teachers in the College of Divinity at Istanbul University, also known as Darülfünun, to teach exegesis there as well. Later, he was transferred to teach at Mütehassisin Medrese where he taught *Ṣaḥīḥ Muslim*. He was also appointed as a ḥadīth teacher at the Süleymaniye Mosque in 1918.

Ṣabrī differed markedly from his peers in that he focused entirely on the traditional Islamic sciences. By the late 19th century, an increasing number of *madrasa* students supplemented their religious education with studies in foreign languages and modern sciences to boost their credentials in an environment of declining appreciation for traditional Islamic scholarship. Ṣabrī possessed none of these supplementary credentials and advanced solely on his exceptional merit in traditional Islamic studies.[14]

In 1898, Ṣabrī was selected to participate in the *Huzur* debates, scholarly conferences held each year during Ramadan in the presence of Sultan Abdülhamid II (r. 1876–1909) (d. 1336/1918).[15] Impressed with Ṣabrī, the youngest among his elite colleagues, the Sultan offered him a job managing his personal library and awarded him state decorations for his intellectual achievements. Ṣabrī became a personal writer for the Sultan and continue participating in the *Huzur* debates until 1913.

Ṣabrī welcomed the revolution of 1908 which saw the establishment of a constitutional order in the Ottoman Empire, and significantly scaled back restrictions on free speech and political activism, of

---

[14] Ibid., at 69.

[15] Ibid., at 70.

which Ṣabrī himself had been a victim in earlier years. "He was a firm supporter of the constitutional system, believing that the majority of Ottoman voters and legislators would support the strengthening of the Islamic character of the state and the special position of the 'ulama' in the polity."[16]

Only a week after the revolution, a group of 113 leading Islamic scholars in Istanbul established the Islamic Scholarly Council (Cem'iyyet-i İlmiyye-i İslamiyye), and unanimously selected Ṣabrī to be their leader, and as editor-in-chief of the group's *Beyanülhak* magazine. Ṣabrī, who to this point had hardly published anything in his life, now wrote prolifically on the social and political problems facing the Empire. He pursued these projects in parallel with teaching positions at some of Istanbul's most prestigious institutions, such as the University of Istanbul's Faculty of Theology, and the Süleymaniye Darülhadis College.[17]

Joined by a group of sympathetic *'ulamā'* working as legislators in the new Ottoman parliament, in 1909 Ṣabrī put forward a resolution calling for the expansion of the *sharī'a*-based Ottoman civil code (the *Mecelle*), hoping to eventually make it the basis for all Ottoman law. The initiative had massive popular support, but was vetoed by the CUP leadership, seriously damaging relations between the Unionists and religious leaders such as Ṣabrī.[18]

Ṣabrī and many other *'ulamā'* became disillusioned by the parliamentary system following the 1912 election. The CUP government used heavy-handed tactics to suppress support for religious factions such as Ṣabrī's, leading them to believe that the Unionists would never willingly relinquish power. Ṣabrī, at this point the spokesman and vice president of the Freedom and Accord Party (Hürriyet ve İtilaf Fırkası), became one of the government's most outspoken public critics.[19] This was vindicated the following year, when the CUP established one-party rule in wake of the loss of the Empire's Balkan territories.[20]

After taking total control of the Ottoman Empire in 1913, the CUP government launched waves of mass arrests against opposition activists in Istanbul; Ṣabrī escaped arrest and fled the country. After months of living as

[16] Ibid., at 72f.
[17] Gharad (n. 11), at 135.
[18] Bein (n. 13), at 75.
[19] Gharad (n. 11), at 137.
[20] Bein (n. 13), at 79f.

a fugitive in France, Egypt and Bosnia, he settled in Romania in 1914. Back in Istanbul, the CUP government stripped him of all titles, confiscated his property, and suspended his citizenship. To survive, he taught at a *madrasa* in Romania, working with the country's Turkish Muslim minority.

Ṣabrī intended to wait out the First World War in exile, watching from afar with dismay as the new government radically reformed the religious establishment to which he had dedicated his life. After Romania entered the war in support of the Entente, the country was invaded and occupied by the Central Powers, including a contingent of the Ottoman army, which arrested Ṣabrī in 1917. He was imprisoned in Bucharest for six months before being sent to stand trial in Istanbul.[21]

Ṣabrī, along with a number of allies, was banished to the remote Anatolian town of Bilecik, where he spent the rest of the war, praying for the downfall of the CUP. He was given an opening in October 1918, when the new sultan Mehmet VI (r. 1918–1922) (d. 1344/1926) declared a general amnesty for political prisoners, and quickly set about rebuilding his network of activist *ʿulamāʾ* in Istanbul. Ṣabrī's allies finally succeeded in gaining control of the government in 1919, with Damat Ferid Pasha (d. 1923) appointed as Grand Vizier, who promptly appointed Ṣabrī as *Şeyhülislam*.[22]

Ṣabrī served in this role for three years, under intense criticism and scrutiny. He was accused in the press of seeking to establish a "*madrasa* regime" (*medrese saltanatı*) and control the Empire. He and his allies pursued their agenda, unperturbed, to undo the CUP's reforms and restore Islamic norms to public life.

Due to frequent disagreements with the government, Ṣabrī resigned and was reinstated as *Şeyhülislam* four times, making his years-long tenure only some eight months in total.[23] Ṣabrī lost many allies towards the end of 1919 for his distrust and animosity towards Mustafa Kemal (d. 1938), then gaining popularity for his military successes against European armies in Anatolia. Ṣabrī believed him to be a Unionist in disguise, who would only continue the old CUP agenda if he gained power, despite protestations of being a sincere Muslim.[24]

His tenure as *Şeyhülislam* lasted until 1922 when political fortunes shifted, and he was forced to flee Turkey to escape arrest by the ascendant nationalist (and ultimately Kemalist) movement.

---

[21] Ibid., at 80f.

[22] Ibid., at 82.

[23] Gharad (n. 11), at 137.

[24] Bein (n. 13), at 84.

Ṣabrī initially fled to Alexandria, Egypt, where he faced considerable abuse for his criticism of Atatürk, then widely perceived as a pan-Islamic hero. He writes that he and his family were pelted with garbage and rotten tomatoes, and lived in poverty and sickness.[25]

Certain Egyptian tabloids even printed rumours that he had "spent two thousand Egyptian pounds on his way from Istanbul," an enormous sum for the time, and had been forced to sell his books and possessions to buy his escape. Others alleged that he was a British spy working against the Muslim cause in Turkey (i.e. Atatürk's movement). Many called for him to be deported from Egypt. Journalists and paparazzi would often wait at his gate and mob him in the streets, asking for his views on the Kemalist revolution and the separation of the Caliphate from political power.

Even scholars and littérateurs in Egypt viciously attacked him for his anti-Kemalist stance. The then *wakīl* of al-Azhar and one of its scholars wrote,

> "Since the time the former *Shaykh al-Islām* published his elaborate article in the Egyptian newspapers, he has been defending himself against accusations of treason against his religion and people, bitter against those who truly fight for the sake of Allāh [i.e. Kemalist Turks]; he has tried to censure and criticise Muslims that favour them, especially the Egyptians who have naturally arrived at this position. They [i.e. the Egyptians] have not honoured him for residing [among them], and are reluctant to let their nation be a refuge for someone who weaves ropes of treachery against Islam and the Muslims."[26]

In 1921, Ṣabrī spent a few months in the Ḥijāz upon invitation from Sharīf Ḥusayn (r. 1916–1924) (d. 1349/1931), but after prolonged illnesses within his family, he was forced to return once again to Egypt. His return proved even more problematic when the poet Aḥmad Shawqī (d. 1351/1932) published a poem in 1922 in *al-Ahrām* that lauded Mustafa Kemal while hurling insults at Mehmet VI as one of the nascent Turkish state's final puppet sultans.

---

[25] Gharad (n. 11), at 138.

[26] Qūsī, Mufriḥ b. Sulaymān al-. *Al-Shaykh Muṣṭafā Ṣabrī Wa Mawqifuhū Min al-Fikr al-Wāfid*. Riyadh, Saudi Arabia: Markaz Malik Fayṣal li 'l-Buḥūth wa 'l-Dirāsāt al-Islāmiyya, 1997, 115–116.

Ṣabrī penned a harsh response in *al-Muqaṭṭam* titled "An Open Address to the Prince of Poets Shawqī Bey." He even copied the metre of Shawqī's poem in his response. This provoked even greater hostility to Ṣabrī in Egypt led by Shawqī's followers, and various newspapers across the country were soon brimming with further insults against the shaykh.

Ṣabrī's final response to these journalists, scholars, poets, and men of letters was eventually compiled in *al-Nakīr 'alā Munkirī 'l-Ni'ma* soon after he relocated to Lebanon. He was pessimistic about the book changing their minds, claiming he wrote it rather "so that it remains a reserve for me in the afterlife and a proof with which I can ultimately take them to account there. And though my tongue may be lacking in Arabic, I ask the honourable readers to pardon me, for the mistakes of the tongue are not like the mistakes of the heart."[27]

In the book, Ṣabrī reminds Egyptians that the Kemalists plainly seek to eradicate the *Sharī'a* from within. He reprimands them for ignoring the corrupt intentions of the Kemalists, and their contempt for Islam. Ultimately, he stresses that the compromised Caliphate, devoid of any authority under their leadership, was of no inherent worth and merely a means by which the enemies of the faith resolved to eradicate popular Islamic piety.[28]

Yet despite prolonged illnesses, hunger, and the constant bombardment of insults and cursing by both the intellectual elite and the masses of Egypt, he was later noted as saying that "this is preferable for me than supporting or praising the oppressors."[29]

Ṣabrī continued travelling for about a decade, writing constantly in condemnation of the new Kemalist regime in his homeland. His troubles would not end in Egypt, however. Upon moving to Romania, where he owned a home, he found that the one to whom he had entrusted the property (a CUP supporter) had stolen it in his absence. From Romania, Ṣabrī made a trip to the Vatican in 1925, boldly petitioning papal authorities to join forces with Muslims against their common enemy of atheistic nationalism, and to help restore the caliphate as a 'moderating force' in the Muslim world.[30]

---

[27] Qūsī, Mufriḥ b. Sulaymān al-. *Muṣṭafā Ṣabrī al-Mufakkir al-Islāmī wa 'l-'Ālim al-'Ālamī wa Shaykh al-Islām fī 'l-Dawlat al-'Uthmāniyya Sābiqan*. Damascus, Syria: Dār al-Qalam, 2006, 140.

[28] Ibid., at 135-145.

[29] Ṣabrī (n. 8), at 17.

[30] Hammond, Andrew. *Late Ottoman Origins of Modern Islamic Thought: Turkish and Egyptian Thinkers on the Disruption of Islamic Knowledge*. Cambridge Studies in Islamic Civilization. Cambridge, UK: Cambridge University Press, 2023, 44.

He travelled to Greece in 1927, remaining there for nearly five years, mainly in Komotini. In 1928 he published a poem titled "I Resign", in which he describes his disgust at the new Turkish state, and offers his resignation from the Turkish nation itself. He writes of his regret that the Turks had not been Arabized in the past, presumably to avoid the possibility of Turkish nationalism separate from Islam.[31] He also began publishing the activist journal *Tomorrow* (*Yarın*). He was eventually expelled by the Greek government from the city at the specific request of Atatürk and relocated to Patras, a predominantly non-Muslim area in the country. Living among non-Muslims over the next few months would leave him in a state of constant agitation.[32] He sought assistance from his Arab colleagues to relocate, but without any help forthcoming, he was forced to emigrate on his own accord. He finally arrived in Egypt on January 20th, 1932 for a third time and would ultimately never leave the country again, even though the Turkish government offered him an amnesty in 1938.

Ṣabrī remained committed to the ideal of Islamic government and society until the end of his life. During his two decades in Egypt, spent mainly in Cairo, he wrote endlessly against secularism, Western culture, and Kemalism. Although his early focus was on his homeland, as years passed Ṣabrī became a keen observer of the Egyptian society in which he was exiled, and wrote against the modernist reform he observed there as well.[33] *Qawlī fī 'l-Mar'a*, a collection of Ṣabrī's writings on modern women's issues and observations of contemporary Egyptian society, was first published on November 8th, 1934 in *al-Fatḥ Magazine*.[34] Ṣabrī's thoughts on the topic quickly gained traction among the magazine's audience and became critically acclaimed among fellow scholars and contemporaries.

Ṣabrī was subsequently encouraged by his close friend and the owner of *al-Fatḥ*, Muḥibb al-Dīn al-Khaṭīb (d. 1389/1969) (a renowned Syrian Salafī scholar and theologian who ultimately settled in Cairo and became known primarily for his anti-Shīʿa polemics), to compile the articles and publish them through his own *al-Maṭbaʿa al-Salafiyya* publishing house in 1935. The work was reprinted over the years numerous times in Beirut, and most recently reproduced in 2019 with Muḥammad Wā'il al-Ḥanbalī's annotations by *Dār al-Lubāb*.

---

[31] Bein (n. 13), at 84.

[32] Gharad (n. 11), at 138.

[33] Hammond (n. 30), at 46.

[34] Qūsī (n. 27), at 294.

Qawlī fī 'l-Mar'a itself tackles a range of modern women's issues, such as feminism, polygamy, free mixing and the veil. The book serves as an apologetic for traditional Islamic practice, using rational proofs and unusually few direct references to the Qur'ān or ḥadīth corpus. Ṣabrī rarely employs any textual Islamic evidences as, understandably, his adversaries would not recognize their intellectual authority.

This is part of Ṣabrī's tragic narrative. What must have truly depressed him (and he does hint at it occasionally throughout the book) was that by the 1930s, even an argument well-founded on Islamic grounds was unpersuasive to a large section of the Egyptian population. He could make it eminently clear to them that what they were doing was un-Islamic, and they might simply persist regardless. Ṣabrī, therefore, grounds his arguments in material realities, the firsthand experiences of his audience, and their desire for happiness in their homes now rather than the promise of salvation and paradise in the Hereafter.

Ṣabrī spent the 1910s and 1920s struggling to preserve and then revive the Islamic caliphate, without success. When this cause appeared doomed for the time being, he shifted focus to moral issues in works such as *Qawlī fī 'l-Mar'a*, rebuilding the foundations of Islamic society for a future political revival.[35]

Exiled from Turkey and the European countries where he had sought refuge, in Egypt Ṣabrī was finally recognized for his status as a major Islamic scholar. His works, from *Qawlī* to *Mawqif al-'Aql*, found wide praise. As the Kemalists' true agenda slowly revealed itself and lost the support of religious Turks, Ṣabrī's opposition to their movement was vindicated, and his critics silenced. He earned the favour of Egyptians and Muslims globally, who often sought his insights on issues of modernity. He was granted a monthly stipend by King Fārūq (r. 1936–1952) (d. 1384/1965), became a teacher to Ḥasan al-Bannā (d. 1368/1949) and the future *Shaykh al-Azhar* Maḥmūd Shaltūt, and was employed by the Egyptian Ministry of Religious Endowments.[36]

---

[35] She writes, "After strenuously trying to hold on to conceptions of the Caliphate rooted in Islamic law, Mustafa Sabri acknowledged that securing its actual implementation had slipped out of his grasp...Yet faced with the surge of secular governance and modern European philosophies, Mustafa Sabri shifted to an even more basic struggle for the rest of his life: preserving the cognitive frameworks of Islam for a new generation of Muslims." See: Hassan, Mona. *Longing for the Lost Caliphate: A Transregional History.* Princeton University Press, 2017, 244.

[36] Gharad (n. 11), at 138.

Ṣabrī passed away Friday, the 12th of March 1373/1954 in Cairo, at the age of 84. His death was announced over Egyptian radio and newspapers, and attended by major national figures. Former *Shaykh al-Azhar* Sayyid Muḥammad al-Khaḍir Ḥusayn (d. 1377/1958), Ottoman prince Şehzade Mahmud Şevket (d. 1392/1973), Grand Mufti of Egypt Ḥasnayn Muḥammad Makhlūf (d. 1410/1990), Mufti of Jerusalem Muḥammad Amīn al-Ḥusaynī (d. 1394/1974), and a delegation from Egyptian president Muḥammad Nagīb (d. 1404/1984) were all present for the funeral procession to al-Kakhyā Mosque, where then *Shaykh al-Azhar* 'Abd al-Raḥmān Tāj (d. 1395/1975) personally led the funeral prayers.[37]

Ṣabrī's Egypt

Ṣabrī's time in Egypt, from his final arrival in the early 1930s to his death in Cairo in 1954, closely aligns with the reign of the country's final monarch, Fārūq I. He arrived in 1932, four years before Fārūq's coronation in 1936, and died in 1954, two years after the army coup of Muḥammad Nagīb and Gamāl 'Abd al-Nāṣir removed Fārūq from power and ended the 150-year rule of the Muḥammad 'Alī dynasty.

The Egypt of Ṣabrī's day was a period of political and social liberality, epitomised by the country's notoriously libertine king, and widespread embrace of Western thought and lifestyles. The perception held by some Muslims today, that all of human history is an inexorable march of progressive liberalisation along Western lines, was perhaps even stronger in the 1930s than at present. Many reformers agitated for doing away with the veil, female participation in the workforce, and relaxed segregation of the sexes in public spaces, all essentially aimed at modelling Egyptian society on that of urban Europe.

The changes Ṣabrī saw in Egypt, as compared with the Ottoman society in which he had grown to adulthood, deeply disturbed him. Indeed, even comparison between Atatürk's Turkey and King Fārūq's Egypt was profoundly depressing; he writes in *Mawqif al-'Aql*:

> "It was my belief in emigrating from Turkey to the Arab lands from which the light of Islam came to us that I could finally relax from fighting against the heretics [in my home country], however I

[37] Ibid., at 142.

found the cultural climate in Egypt was also attuned to those of Western thought and tendency, and this was harder on me than [seeing] the state of modern Turkey in the face of that [same tendency]. It also tore [my heart] to recognize that my Arab brothers preferred this [new] Turkey over the old Muslim Turkey, and I saw them plunging headlong into imitation of the West, even preceding the Turks in being seduced by it. The revolution which was so violent in Turkey took form more calmly among them, through influence and reformation inside al-Azhar."[38]

Fewer and later marriages became endemic in early 20th century Egypt, owing to the country's economic troubles and the new material aspirations of Egyptians. In mid-19th century Egypt, the median marriage age for girls was 13.8, while a century later, it had risen to 18.6.[39] A crisis of mass-bachelorhood took hold as men could not afford the new dowry standards, which were inspired by Western lifestyles financially unattainable for Egyptian men. Feminists and conservatives both decried excessive dowries in this period. The mass of listless, lonely bachelors fuelled the emergence in Cairo of a lively network of nightclubs, bars, brothels and parties popular with middle-class Egyptians in the 1920s and 1930s, and made the city the most glamorous, Westernised destination in the Middle East.[40] Cairo attracted a regular stream of visiting Western celebrities, often invited by King Fārūq himself to his lavish parties.[41]

The feminist movement in Egypt began during the Nahḍa period with the publication of Qāsim Amīn's *Taḥrīr al-Mar'a* (Women's Liberation) in 1899, and had grown highly influential by the 1930s. It began principally among Egypt's religious minorities; out of the fifteen early feminist women's magazines published in Egypt in the late 19th century, only one, possibly two, were actually founded and written in by Muslim women, with the remainder founded by Egyptian Christians and Jews.[42] Aside from Ṣabrī's own criticisms of Amīn in *Qawlī fī 'l-Mar'a,* Amīn's book was sharply contested by the *'ulamā'* of his day, such as Muḥammad Aḥmad Ḥasnayn al-Būlāqī (d. 1343/1925) in his work *al-Jalīs al-Anīs*, Ḥusayn al-Rifā'ī in *Khulāṣat*

[38] Ṣabrī, Muṣṭafā. *Mawqif al-'Aql wa 'l-'Ilm.* Beirut, Lebanon: Dār Iḥyā' al-Turāth al-'Arabī, 1981, 1/23., al-Qūsī (n. 27), at 151-152.

[39] Kholoussy, Hanan. *For Better, For Worse: The Marriage Crisis That Made Modern Egypt.* Stanford, California: Stanford University Press, 2010, 56.

[40] Ibid., at 40.

[41] Stadiem, William. *Too Rich: The High Life and Tragic Death of King Farouk.* New York: Carroll & Graf Publishers, 1991, 219–220.

[42] Ghoussoub, Mai. "Feminism—or the Eternal Masculine—in the Arab World." *New Left*, no. 161 (1987): 10.

al-Adab, Muṣṭafā al-Ghalāyīnī (d. 1363/1944) in *Naẓarāt fī 'l-Sufūr wa 'l-Ḥijāb*, Muṣṭafā Najā (d. 1350/1932) in *Risāla fī Mashrū'iyyat al-Ḥijāb*, 'Abd al-Raḥmān al-Ḥimṣī in *Risālat al-Fatā wa 'l-Fatāt*,[43] as well as the leading Egyptian industrialist Muḥammad Ṭal'at Ḥarb (d. 1360/1941) in his *Tarbiyyat al-Mar'a wa 'l-Ḥijāb* as well as *Faṣl al-Khiṭāb fī 'l-Mar'a wa 'l-Ḥijāb*, among others.[44]

Under the old order of gender relations in Egypt, women wore veils in public and minimised their time outside the home, except working (and typically poor) women for whom these luxuries were impractical. The dominant style in this period was a simple white veil, which originated in Istanbul. Discarding the veil became one of the main thrusts of Egypt's feminist movement led by the likes of Hudā Sha'rāwī, founder of the women's journal *L'Egyptienne*, and Malak Ḥifnī Nāṣif (d. 1918), founder of *al-Nisā'iyyāt*.

Under the influence of Sha'rāwī, Nāṣif, and male advocates of feminist ideas such as Qāsim Amīn, a trend towards unveiling among elite Egyptian women had begun. Western dress became popular among the upper classes, minority women and later Muslim women stopped veiling outside the home, and young girls never started.[45] King Fārūq himself made a strong statement by taking his wife Farīda with him everywhere he went, completely unveiled and in Western dress.[46] While elite Egyptian women inspired by the feminist movement began to abandon the veil, it became for their opposition a symbol of loyalty to the old Ottoman order, and defiance against Western colonial modernity.[47]

The campaign for unveiling in Egypt unfolded over decades. The public, national feminist movement for desegregation (of the sexes) and unveiling began in 1923, although the likes of Qāsim Amīn and other male women's liberationists held full unveiling to be 'premature' at that time, advocating a more methodical, patient strategy.[48] This gradualist approach was specifically identified by conservative critics such as Ṣabrī, who worried about its likely effectiveness.

---

[43] Fahmī, Māhir Ḥasan. *Qāsim Amīn*. Cairo, Egypt: Wizārat al-Thaqāfa wa 'l-Irshād al-Qawmī, 1963, 164–165.

[44] Muqaddam, Muḥammad Aḥmad Ismā'īl al-. *'Awdat Al-Ḥijāb*. Vol. 10. Riyadh, Saudi Arabia: Dār al-Ṭayyiba, 2007, 50-51.

[45] Baron, Beth. *Egypt as a Woman: Nationalism, Gender, and Politics*. Berkeley and Los Angeles, California: University of California Press, 2005, 35f.

[46] Stadiem (n. 40), at 165.

[47] Baron (n. 44), at 35.

[48] Ibid., at 14f.

Another of Ṣabrī's chief concerns in *Qawlī fī 'l-Mar'a* is the normalisation of free-mixing between the sexes. Segregation of the sexes in Egypt prior to the advent of the feminist movement was a sign of honour, available to upper and middle-class women not required to work, but not for lower-class women compelled to do so.[49] Marriage shifted at the turn of the century from being primarily a contractual relationship (maintenance in exchange for child-rearing, homemaking and marital relations) to a partnership, at least for Western-educated Egyptian men. They sought educated wives, intellectual partners, similar to the women they had met in Paris or London during their studies.

Qāsim Amīn thought it a waste for Egypt to have so many cultivated young men lacking suitable female partners. He, therefore, proposed ending women's seclusion and lack of education, which was, he assured his audience, not a blind imitation of Europe, but a return to original Islamic values.[50] Cultivated young Egyptian men with experience abroad also began to reject traditional arranged marriages; they demanded they be allowed to meet and mingle with their potential spouses, as was done in Europe.[51] Kholoussy notes that this argument was something of a farce; even those conservatives who supported seclusion allowed for chaperoned meetings to determine compatibility.[52]

Another key issue of women's changing role in Egyptian society was their education. Egyptian feminists of the early 20th century argued for female education on the grounds that it would strengthen the Egyptian nation, and by extension Muslims generally. Malak Ḥifnī Nāṣif "opposed the aping of all things European and was critical of the *alafranka* style (in emulation of Europeans or "Franks") of youth in her day, but she still found much to admire and worthy of emulation in European 'knowledge, vigour, perseverance, and love of work,' and in their teaching methods."[53] The ideal woman of the period, in the eyes of critics across the social spectrum, was balanced between East and West. Educated, but not so much as to corrupt her domestic and obedient character. Indeed, as an anonymous author in the journal *al-Hilāl* writes in 1897,

---

[49] Badran, Margot. "The Feminist Vision in the Writings of Three Turn-of-the-Century Egyptian Women." *Bulletin (British Society for Middle Eastern Studies)* 15, no. 1/2 (1988): 12.

[50] Kholoussy (n. 39), at 50.

[51] Ibid., at 52.

[52] Ibid., at 53.

[53] Cuno, Kenneth M. *Modernizing Marriage: Family, Ideology and Law in Nineteenth- and Early Twentieth-Century Egypt.* First Edition. Gender and Globalization. Syracuse, N.Y.: Syracuse University Press, 2015, 141.

> "If the Eastern young woman restricts herself in the customs of the foreigners [limiting herself] to seeking knowledge, strengthening the intellect, and gaining from the talent of providence and household administration, remaining modest and energetic; and [she] distances [herself] from carousing, opulence, playing, and dancing, then she will glean the advantages of the East and the West..."[54]

The feminists stressed nationalist values in their advocacy for women's education and employment; with more educated and working Egyptian women, they argued, the need for foreign nurses and nannies employed in upper-class homes and their alien cultural influences would be eliminated.

The feminists also argued for the social upgrade of women through education and employment as a means to get them out of the working situations which put them beneath men, and made them sexually exploitable. If a woman were a man's professional equal he would be unable to exploit her, or so the argument went. Here, they shrewdly appealed to religious sentiment and positioned themselves as allies with the conservatives against sexual impropriety in modern Egypt.[55]

On the flip side, many Egyptian men and social critics lamented the Westernization of Egyptian women in this period, facilitated in large part by government schools, as a reason why they were unappealing to men. Sayyid Ḥamdī, noting all the foregoing calls to educate Egypt's ignorant women, said men were at fault; they had demanded educated wives, but now did not like them.[56] Many Egyptian families therefore were hesitant to educate their daughters, fearing they could become haughty and undesirable for marriage.

ʿAbd Allāh al-Nadīm (d. 1314/1896), a renowned Egyptian poet and political activist, elsewhere expressly notes the problematic connection of language competency to women's desirability in marriage. In his publication *Girls' School* (1892) al-Nadīm presents fictional discussions between young Egyptian women studying in modern schools, through whom he decries the

[54] "The Eastern Young Woman at the End of the Nineteenth Century." *al-Hilāl* 6, no. 5 (1897), 173-74.
[55] Badran (n. 48), at 16f.
[56] Kholoussy (n. 39), at 63.

practice of teaching women European languages, dancing, and musical instruments.[57]

Family formation thus became delayed in Egypt by the pursuit of years-long higher education, both among men and women. This was advocated by both liberals and nationalists, not so much for the benefits to Egyptian women as to the Egyptian nation. Anṭūn al-Gamayyil (d. 1948) in *The Girl and the Home* writes:

> "For the happiness of the family and the future of the community [*al-umma*], and in the noble name of marriage and the majesty of motherhood, the young woman's education must be among the most important and exalted matters."[58]

Qāsim Amīn wanted women to be educated primarily to make them better mothers, and thought primary education was sufficient for women.[59] It is interesting to note that Qāsim Amīn's education policy is even more restrictive than that of modern Afghanistan, which attracts so much criticism today. One wonders how Qāsim Amīn and other similar contemporary reformists would feel about what has resulted from their activism across various Muslim societies today.

It is a testament to Ṣabrī's incredible foresight that he dedicated such time and attention to the changes he observed taking place among Egypt's elite, when in his own time they concerned such a minority of women. Those Egyptian women with access to new lifestyles, Western education and feminist ideas were a narrow class of upper- and middle-class women living in Cairo and Alexandria. For the great mass of working women in the small cities and villages of Egypt, family life and customs changed little in this period.[60] Nonetheless, Ṣabrī correctly perceived the course on which Muslim societies were moving, and devoted his full attention to the pressing issues of his day. He was a remarkable man who made vast efforts on behalf of the *Umma*.

---

[57] Herrera, Linda. "'The Soul of a Nation': Abdallah Nadim and Education Reform in Egypt (1845-1896)." *Mediterranean Journal of Education Studies* 7, no. 1 (2002): 11ff.

[58] Russell, Mona L. Creating the New Egyptian Woman: Consumerism, Education, and National Identity, 1863–1922. New York, NY: Palgrave Macmillan, 2004, 145.

[59] Kholoussy (n. 39), at 60.

[60] Russell (n. 57), at 2.

A WORD ON TRANSLITERATION

Arabic words and names have been transliterated according to the standard academic system of Arabic-English translation, with diacritics. Some names have minor deviations from this system to accommodate more common usages. Turkish names have been rendered as they would be written according to the modern Turkish latin alphabet, with one exception: Ṣabrī himself. We have decided to make Ṣabrī an exception to the other Turks mentioned in this book as we humbly imagine that is what he would prefer. In addition to his explicit 'resignation' from the Turkish nation itself, Shaykh Muṣṭafā Ṣabrī absolutely opposed the Kemalist programme of replacing the Arabic script of Ottoman Turkish with an adapted latin script, and as anyone who reads his original writings can attest, was an extraordinarily articulate Arabophone. Ṣabrī was more at home in the Arabic-literate intellectual culture of the late Ottoman Empire than the Westernised Turkish Republic which replaced it, and so we have chosen to render his name according to Arabic, rather than Turkish convention. We have also added sub-headings to the book not originally included by Ṣabrī, to break up the text and ease reading.

Muzzammil al-Nadwī & Junayd Greer

A TRANSLATION OF *QAWLĪ FĪ 'L-MAR'A*

Introduction

In the name of Allāh, the Most Compassionate, the Most Merciful,
All praise is due to Allāh, Lord of the worlds, and may blessings and peace be upon our master Muḥammad and his family and companions.

To begin; the issue of women has from a time not far [from our own] been the greatest point of distinction between the East and the West, and between Islam and other religions in society. This difference is so great that one could hardly imagine the West would find anyone among the Eastern Muslims, who are known for their protective jealousy (*ghayra*),[61] to follow them in the exposure of their women, even if they were followed in other things. Alas, unfortunately, the Eastern Muslim man's protective jealousy over his women has faded, as has his jealousy over his religion. And perhaps the fading of the former was worldly compensation from Allāh for the loss of the latter.

Thus, whoever looks toward what is manifest in the West would surmise that its people worship the woman, elevating her worth to that [exalted] degree. And in contrast to that, the Eastern woman would be considered unfortunate, deprived of [her] liberties. However, the reality is that Westerners, and those among us who follow them, only pursue their idle desires in worshipping women. Modern man's exaltation of the woman

---

[61] Protective jealousy, pronounced as *al-ghayra* in Arabic, refers to a sense of honour (*al-anafa*) and zeal (*al-ḥamiyya*) felt by an individual (both male and female) in maintaining their rights, loved ones, and property. It is also defined more specifically as displeasure felt by an individual, more acutely noticed in men, when having to share their sole rights with others. While it can be felt towards any right of a sacred nature, it is most often associated with protective jealousy between spouses, moreso of a man towards his wife (and the women of his household), and his outbursts of anger (*thawrān al-ghaḍab*) when he feels his rights over them threatened. Scholars state that this emotion was divinely placed within people as a means of preserving family and lineage (*nasab*), the lack of which would lead to societal chaos and decay. There are numerous other narrations that speak of protective jealousy within the Prophet (ﷺ)–manifested in protecting and preserving the religion beyond anyone else–as well as Allāh possessing this right on His slaves (that they should not associate others with Him in worship, or that they should disobey Him). See: al-Rāzī, Muḥammad. *Mukhtār al-Ṣiḥāḥ*. Beirut: al-Maktaba al-'Aṣriyya, 1999, 232., al-Rāghib al-Aṣfahānī, al-Ḥusayn. *al-Dharī'a ilā Makārim al-Sharī'a*. Beirut: Dār al-Kutub al-'Ilmiyya, 1980, 238., al-Kafawī, Ayyūb. *al-Kulliyyāt*. Beirut: Mu'assasat al-Risāla, 671. al-'Asqalānī, Ibn Ḥajar. *Fatḥ al-Bārī bi Sharḥ Ṣaḥīḥ al-Bukhārī*. Beirut: Dār al-Ma'rifa, 1959-1960, 9/320.

and his promotion of her over himself, however, is nothing but false flattery, intended to deceive her and make her a vessel of petty amusement and play.

Just as removing a woman from her private quarters and covering means pulling her down from her fortified throne into the markets of disgrace, her engagement in men's work–which is counted as her attaining the rights of "empowerment" to become equal with men–is nothing but laying upon her the hardship of life so tough that even Eastern men remain yet to adopt it properly, much less their women.

Her bearing of these burdens comes from her being engaged with men, so it is not difficult to imagine that her protection from coercion will be predicated on men pardoning her and not taking advantage of her femininity–and therein lies the woman's disgrace. The Eastern woman used to be the best supporter of man, who would help him in his home, participating with him in all aspects of [domestic] life. As either wife or mother, she was the queen of her family estate. What we say here concerns the Eastern Muslim woman who *does* possess her rights, and should not be confused with some unfortunate wives married to oppressive husbands who are cruel to their families; what is necessary [in such cases] is to rectify their affairs within the boundaries of Islamic civil society, and the divine law (*al-shar'*) is fully capable of punishing such oppressors, whoever they may be.

So this woman, weak in bodily faculties–as attested to in Plato's writings on women's equality with men,[62] used [today] by advocates of the modern woman,[63] and which we will elaborate further in the article, "*Veiling and Unveiling*"–if it is persecution to exist as man's companion, his domestic helper, as is the station of the Eastern Muslim woman, then her persecution and subjugation becomes all the more pronounced when she engages [with man] in both domestic life and in competition for [financial] livelihood.

She has no satisfactory escape from this persecution except to become a mere diversion and plaything for men. So those who work for the "freedom" of the Eastern woman, [in becoming] like her Western sister, further tarnish her with this latter state of degradation, all while claiming she has been relieved of the [earlier] persecution faced by women. [They

---

[62] This equality between the sexes, one promoted by modern proponents of feminism, was a proposition Plato otherwise held, though he too admits certain present differences between the two, including physical capabilities. See: 'Abd al-Fattāḥ, Imām. *Aflāṭūn wa 'l-Mar'a.* Cairo: Maktaba Madbouly, 1995-1996.

[63] Plato writes in Book V of *The Republic* that men and women are essentially of the same nature, except for their physical strength. They should consequently be given the same education and take up largely the same work. See: Plato. *The Republic of Plato.* Translated by Allan Bloom. Second edition. New York, NY: HarperCollins Publishers, 1991, 130.

are] not dissimilar to those advocates of unveiling who try to ennoble the woman by allowing foreign men–those who see and freely mix with her–to compete with her husband for her [attention].

In our understanding, the woman's physical weakness, which our opponents concede, along with men's lust for her out of their human nature (*fiṭra*), her inability to be completely independent of them, and the lasting effect on her from her interaction with men, all combine to make it impossible for her to be totally independent in life.

It also makes it incumbent upon her not to remain alone, and to not be susceptible to [the scheming of] men. She should remain restricted to just one man, and remove herself from whatever prevents this dependency [on him], near or far.

This is a summary of these two articles: *The Foundations of Polygamy*, and *Unveiling and Veiling*; two issues that continue being debated between those trying to hold onto their religion and traditions, and those whose bodies are in the East, but whose hearts lie in the West. The reader will realise [after studying] the content of these two articles that reason, tradition, and virtue all support the former. Heedless, lustful desires blind the views of the latter. Binding their necks are shackles of blind imitation (*taqlīd*) on which is inscribed, "We found our role models and exemplars (*qibla*), the Westerners, following a particular path, and we follow in their footsteps."

Do not think that the first group follows their forefathers blindly, saying, "Indeed, we found our forefathers upon a religion...etc.," [*al-Zukhruf*: 22-23] while the latter walks the path of reason and reflection. Had they [i.e. the latter group] stated the former, they would have been partially excused as blind imitation of forefathers would have been closer to [true] guidance than blindly imitating the foreigners. Their imitation is entirely blind, while the former's imitation has [at least some] reason and virtue as support.

Muṣṭafā Ṣabrī
Former *Şeyhülislam* of the Ottoman Empire

THE BASIS OF POLYGAMY

It is well-known that the question of *the woman* remains among the most pressing of modern times, and the greatest criterion between the Western and Islamic civilisations.

Acknowledging the Permissibility of Polygamy is Necessary for a Muslim

Polygamy remains the first issue on which Islam is often criticised, and the most popular of those weak points on which the gaze of Westerners, and those Muslims who view matters through their lens, lingers. Even if some of them [i.e. Westernised Muslims] are engaged in apologetics on its behalf, the furthest they can reach is to argue that polygamy is not necessary in Islam, and that it is confined to the historical conditions which allowed the possibility of its existence.[64]

What goes above such people, however, is that:

- The recognition that the permissibility of polygamy is at its very root necessary for the believer, and
- Its stipulations do not make it impossible [in any era], otherwise its legislation would have been superfluous and vain. Furthermore, the Companions who acted on it would have been seeking something impossible.

I have discussed this issue exhaustively in my book which I wrote thirteen years ago in Turkish.[65] Seeing that writers in some newspapers have once again taken up interest in this issue in recent times, I have decided to express my own view [once again].

---

[64] An early 20th-century Muslim thinker who advanced this view was Rashīd Riḍā. In Riḍā's view, the ideal marital arrangement is monogamy, however polygamy is permitted as a dispensation in extraordinary circumstances. See: Riḍā, Muḥammad Rashīd. *Fatāwā al-Imām Muḥammad Rashīd Riḍā.* Edited by Ṣalāḥ al-Dīn al-Munajjid and Yūsuf Khūrī. Vol. 1. 6 vols. Beirut, Lebanon: Dār al-Kitāb al-Jadīd, 2005, 1/119-125.

[65] Ṣabrī is referring here to his work *Dini Müceddidler* (Reformers of the Religion). In the work, he responds to many doubts presented by Muslim reformers, and the adoption of various Western principles. The final chapter of the work pertains to polygamy. For more on the book, see the introduction.

What Islam seeks in marriage and marital life is the continuation of lineage and the fulfilling of physical human needs for intimacy in a legislated, managed way.

None of the other religions or laws of civilisation are too far from seeking these same two goals. It is understood that religion and [sound] reason are congruent in turning to legislate intimacy, as opposed to leaving it unlegislated.

When the need of any man for the companionship of a woman arises, then there is no way to achieve that, [which is considered suitable] in [sound] reasoning or from revelation, except through its pre-legislated path, i.e. marriage.

It must be acknowledged, however, that there are men in this world who cannot suffice with one spouse alone, and actively seek others. Recognising the conceptual need for polygamy is [unavoidable and] necessary, unless one **i)** deviates from reason and revelation and permits fornication, or **ii)** ignores the realities [of the nature of sex] and denies the existence of married men who resort to fornication or **iii)** for those whose minds cannot grasp [the simple fact] that prohibiting polygamy naturally entails that some men will fall into fornication.

Just this amount of discussion is enough as dominating proof for those who hold polygamy to be necessary, and suffices in refuting the proofs of those who reject it, without need to prolong the discussion.

I will persist, throughout the length of [this] debate, comparing between marriage (*al-nikāḥ*) and fornication (*al-sifāḥ*), and will [always] prefer polygamy for those whose desires [would otherwise] drive them to enjoying women impermissible for them in the sight of the divine law, whether through coitus, kissing, embracing, or [merely] looking at them. And I will [continue] specifically highlighting those thieves–those that rob [women's] dignity–by placing them at the point of divergence between the supporters of polygamy and its opponents.[66]

Islam is chaste. It does not permit men to enjoy [anyone] other than their wives, with whom they have a legitimate contract. So if they feel a need for [further] intimacy [from an additional wife], it should not come except through its proper channel. They should seek this [intimacy] with

---

[66] Ṣabrī is stating that where people argue and disagree on the issue, he would put forward these individuals as proof for the position that polygamy is necessary otherwise it brings about their existence.

another contract recognized in divine law, such that people know: this woman is the second *wife* of this man.

Islam is not content putting men and women in illicit relationships; making women prey for the poacher, or playthings for the corrupt.

Second wife! Yes, this term is heavy on the tongues of those who are enthralled (*al-maftūnīn*), mesmerised into changing their intellects and social behaviours to match those of the Westerners, who purchase depravity and perversion at the price of guidance.

Oh how I wonder! How do they find [the term "second wife"] when compared with "casual sex partner (*al-maznī bihā*)", which they euphemistically refer to as a "girlfriend" trying to mask her disgrace and minimise her shame?! The divine law does not recognize this [type of] "friendship", nor is it openly announced in society; rather it is whispered among the friends, i.e. the fornicators themselves.

Does a Woman Prefer her Husband to Marry Another or to Have an Affair

I became astonished when I read what one author wrote in this regard, "were we to ask any woman, 'would you prefer to see your husband marry a second woman, or only have an affair with her?' she would say 'I would rather that he have an affair with a thousand women other than me, because [eventually] he will return to his senses, and to me alone.'"

My response: What does it say about the status of a woman who prefers to be the wife of a man who has affairs with a thousand women, as opposed to being the wife of a chaste man?

What is the worth of what this depraved, fallen woman says? She whose senses have crumbled to such an extent? And what is the worth of her appraisal of men, while she holds chastity in such low regard?

Is it this type of woman that the writer places in a position of judgement, and whose statement he presents as a decisive factor in important social issues like this?

Could any man say [the same]? That 'I would not stop my wife from having an affair so long as she returns to her senses and to me'?!

Twenty-five years ago, I wrote a poem (*qaṣīda*) in Turkish and published it in some Istanbul newspapers, challenging the blind followers of the West who loathed the basis of polygamy. The subject of [this poem] was a conversation between two women, wherein I described such a woman–in the words of one of the interlocutors–[who could be] displeased by her husband marrying another woman while taking no issue if he has affairs with [other] women, as being a 'two-horned woman.'[67]

And were you to ask the author who, at the beginning of his article, describes those who oppose polygamy as the bearers of civilisation: Is such a woman, whom he informs us would tolerate a thousand affairs such that she would grow a thousand horns, included among them?

The root of the writer's laxity in attributing such a statement to any woman[68] is that he seeks to spread corruption among men, [and succeeds,] such that this has become a pervasive issue. It has [now] become a very minor thing for women to choose corrupt men as husbands, and easier for men to speak favourably of this choice as well [i.e. to prefer infidelity over polygamy].

The writer counts the man with children from two wives as a sinner; as though the children of the second wife were enemies that he brings into the family. And yet the author does not consider him sinful if he brings in a bastard [instead].

Maybe he overlooks it similarly to how the wife overlooks the mistress and [her husband's] children from her. Or [perhaps] he [the writer] pretends they do not exist, as she does, because they are unknown to her and society, and [in that way] are nonexistent. The view of Islam is accurate in seeing fornication as the murder and execution of a soul, and so it compensates it in kind.

As for what he mentions of the quarrelling of the paternal step-siblings (*banī 'l-'allāt*) amongst themselves, then the root of that is the lack of a necessary religious upbringing (*tarbiyya*).

And what would the writer say of maternal step-siblings (*banī 'l-akhyāf*), with regards to the hostility that could possibly arise among them?[69]

---

[67] What Ṣabrī means here is that some women would rather see their husbands having secret affairs with other women, as opposed to giving them the honour of being their wives as well. In order to preserve her own status, she would deprive others of it as well. In reality, her sense of protective jealousy over her husband is weak, and her protective jealousy over her public status as an exclusive wife means more to her, even at the cost of the dignity of other women.

[68] That is, making it seem like affairs are a minor issue (especially in comparison to something like polygamy).

[69] It should be highlighted that the potential for strife between step-siblings also exists for full siblings, but should not constitute a concern preventing marriage in the first place. Similarly, strife can also occur between maternal half-siblings. Would those protesting polygamy, who cite this potential strife as a reason for their opposition to the practice, be consistent and demand that divorcees and widows remain unmarried in order to avoid this pitfall? Or do the benefits of marriage, in general, far outweigh its potential shortcomings?

Could we possibly imagine that the law would establish a standard practice of prohibiting a widow or divorcee from remarriage so that she does not give birth to children who would become hostile to those of her first husband, as is assumed in the legal standard which prohibits polygamy?

Moreover, could a legal precedent be imagined which prevented men, widowers, or divorcees, from marrying a second time, seeing as they could produce paternal step-siblings, and inevitably give rise to conflict between them [and their earlier children]?

The Ills of Fornication are Greater than the Effects of Polygamy

It becomes obvious that the opponents of polygamy, who count up all the social ills found in a polygamous society, can be countered at every step with the [far greater] woes caused by fornication. Furthermore, it is impossible for the sound mind to prefer fornication over polygamy, or prefer its calamities to what results [from polygamy].[70]

Dr. Mazhar Osman Bey's Statement on Polygamy

It is for that reason that the renowned Turkish doctor Mazhar Osman Bey (d. 1951),[71] who famously specialises in psychological and neurological disorders, states in his book *Spiritual Medicine*:

> "Sufficiency with one wife (*monogamie*), as observed in Europe, is [merely] a false display of [what the French term] "*etiquette*," distant from reality. It has become apparent that it does not prevent corruption. It is preferable that we respect our religion's

[70] In his edition of *Qawlī fī 'l-Mar'a*, Wā'il al-Ḥanbalī notes here that "As the Prophet (ﷺ) informed us, '...Immorality never appears among a people to such an extent that they commit it openly, except that plagues and diseases that were never known among the predecessors will spread among them...'" *Sunan Ibn Mājah* (4019) Chapter: Punishments. See: Ṣabrī, Muṣṭafā. *Qawlī fī 'l-Mar'a wa Muqāranatuhū bi Aqwāl Muqallidat al-Gharb.* Edited by Muḥammad Wā'il al-Ḥanbalī. Istanbul, Türkiye: Dār al-Lubāb, 2019, 32 fn.1.

[71] Dr. Mazhar Osman Bey, whose full name was Yūsuf Maẓhar 'Uthmān b. 'Uthmān Zuhdī, was an accomplished psychiatrist of the late Ottoman period and a member of the Turkish Neuropsychiatric Society. He published a psychiatric journal from 1919 until his death in 1951, titled *İstanbul Seririyatı* (Istanbul Clinics). He also established the Turkish Green Crescent (established as *Hilâl-i Ahdar Cemiyeti*), a non-profit organisation seeking to curb smoking, alcohol, and drug use among the youth of Istanbul in 1920 under the patronage of *Şeyhülislam* İbrahim Hayderizade (d. 1352/1933). The organisation continues operations today as *Türk Yeşilayı*. He also established a hospital specialising in mental health issues in the Bakırköy municipality of Istanbul. The hospital, named after him, continues operations today. See: *al-Mawsū'a al-Islāmiyya al-Turkiyya* (42/189), op cit Wā'il al-Ḥanbalī, 32; Artvinli, Fatih, Şahap Erkoç, and Fulya Kardeş. "Two Branches of the Same Tree: A Brief History of Turkish Neuropsychiatric Society (1914–2016)." *Noro Psikiyatr Ars* 54, no. 4 (2017): 364–71.

> legislated [system of] polygamy, rather than ignoring how this expansiveness necessarily entails the present [state of] corruption and depravity [found today]."

The opposing writer says, concerning the ratio of men and women, that, "If a war breaks out, and a large number of men were to die in it, it would become possible for us to return to our religion and establish polygamy with the changing times." I [for my part] implore him to "return to his religion" without delay.

I wrote in my aforementioned book:[72] Based on the number of women being greater than that of men, or the reduction of their number through wars, or some men's lack of interest in marriage, or the desire of some single women to marry [already] married men, or any number of reasons; it is possible for there to be a woman who desires to be the second wife of a man, and for polygamy to be within the realm of possibility.

And [the very existence of] such a woman is sufficient to be considered an addition [to the number of women over men] when tallying their numbers. If this woman was not to be found, then there would be no place for polygamy, nor for people to complain about it.

The Presence of Sex Workers Indicates That There Are More Women Than Men

While my defence of polygamy primarily relates to fornication and immorality, I can also prove that there are more women than men. Without taking the issue to distant valleys,[73] [one can simply] highlight [this surplus by acknowledging] the presence of certain women in every city who live by selling their honour. I need not prove that these women are a surplus over men in every town in which they are found; they are obviously present as a surplus. It is incumbent upon men who are compelled [by their lust] to be with them, to [instead] marry them [i.e. these women]. Whether they are already married or single, they should make what they pay for the price of their chastity into maintenance for the family.

I oblige them to do so. This will not please the opponents [of polygamy], however, because they seek to position men such that they can

---

[72] Ṣabrī is referring here once again to his work *Dini Müceddidler* (Reformers of the Religion). See: Ṣabrī (n. 70), at 33.

[73] i.e., one need not think too far.

easily replace one woman with another. Thus it becomes apparent that the objectors [to polygamy] are displeased by the limitations which polygamy [in Islam] guarantees, despite their protests [to the contrary]. It is in this vein that one European writer says, "Muslims may lay with up to four women, but Westerners, who consider themselves more civilised than they, may lay with whatever number they please."

Opponents, startled by my position, retort, "how can every man marry the one with whom he seeks to fornicate? Perhaps she is a prostitute, living at an open or hidden brothel, and opening her door to whoever knocks. How can honour and such a marriage coincide?"

Yet I will only add to their surprise, by saying that marriage does not lower human dignity as much as fornication does. And no matter how high a man's dignity, he will plunge into the depths [of degradation] for the woman with whom he wants to fornicate. Marriage, however, does not diminish a man's dignity and honour, but rather raises up the woman and saves her from dishonouring herself."

The Woman and the Man with Regard to Polygamy

As for the writer's statement that, "it is a woman's right to singly possess her husband and his love, and that she should say to him in public, 'if you attach another woman to your chest, then I will attach another man to mine, for [as they say,] an eye for an eye and a tooth for a tooth,'" it bears remembering that he also described a woman who would rather her husband fornicate with a thousand women rather than take a second wife, as we have commented on previously. When you bring together and synthesise these two positions, the result will be that:

That woman whose husband fornicates with a thousand women will herself, lex talionis, fornicate with a thousand men. This is despite her permitting him those countless affairs, preferring that over him marrying another. Perhaps she prefers that he fornicate rather than marry [a second wife] because it makes it possible for her to retaliate [in kind]. Because she cannot say, "if he marries after me a second, then I shall take a second husband," because neither the law nor her human nature (*fiṭra*) allows this, and because her uterus cannot combine children from two men without the mixture of lineage.[74] As for a man, it is possible for him to accompany many

[74] Meaning, the paternity of the child would be unknown.

women and sire many children without any confusion in their parentage, and this is one of the most apparent distinctions between man and woman.

It is established that the corruption of husbands provokes their wives and leads to their corruption. As for the existence of corrupt men, this is a fact impossible to deny through concealment, in fact, it is impossible to conceal altogether. [Instead], it is obligatory to correct the conduct [of such people] with polygamy – [an institution] which Muslims have come to forget since corruption took its place.

And if someone asks, "how can we prevent widespread corruption in the land by reviving polygamy? It is not even the case that all the corrupt people are married [to begin with] such that we may marry them to a second."

The response to that is the corrupt person–or in preferable expression: he who sees himself liable to fall into corruption–if he is single, should marry. And if he is married, then he should marry a second, and a third, and a fourth, until he attains [sexual] sufficiency. And if he cannot be satisfied with four, and desires a fifth, then he should divorce one and marry that fifth.

If all this is considered playing around with one's family and household, well, **I would respond** that [such playing around and all it entails] is still better than corruption [and infidelity].

Have mercy on me! Some evils are not as bad as others.[75]

And what [would I say] if they were to ask me about the fountains of wealth necessary for [all] these marriages? I would show them the fountains of wealth spent in corruption, and that is [certainly far] more...

The Veil, Polygamy, and Simplifying Divorce Prevents Corruption

Additionally, returning to our faith in covering women and not allowing them to mix with men lowers sexual appetites, and these two

[75] This verse is taken from the poem (*qaṣīda*) of the pre-Islamic poet Ṭarafa b. al-'Abd (d. 569 AD). In the first part of the verse, Ṭarafa says, "Abū Mundhir! You have annihilated [us], so spare those that remain..." He composes these verses addressing the pre-Islamic Arabian king 'Amr b. Hind (d. 569 AD), recognized by the teknonym Abū Mundhir, who had sworn an oath to kill him and others from his people. After killing some others, Ṭarafa stated these words to the king and they would also serve as an incitement to his people to avenge his death. See: al-A'lam al-Shantamarī, Yūsuf. *Dīwān Ṭarafa b. al-'Abd Sharḥ al-A'lam al-Shantamarī.* Lebanon: al-Mu'assasat al-'Arabiyya li 'l-Dirāsāt wa 'l-Nashr–Dār al-Thaqāfat wa 'l-Funūn, 169.

things complement polygamy in preventing corruption. In fact, they may even suffice one from [needing to partake in] polygamy in the first place, because polygamy has been placed in rivalry and competition with corruption.

The third medicine–against the sickness of corruption–is to make divorce easier to a certain extent, as we have previously indicated, because Islam legislated divorce as it legislated marriage.

However, the modern trend which has become the norm in the Muslim world has made divorce impossible, such that a Muslim man unhappy with his partner is forced to accompany her for his whole life. When he leaves home, his eyes roam over all the women of the world, and he sighs deeply with resignation, and perhaps even fornicates. He bears its [i.e., fornication's] sin, but is unable to bear the shame of divorcing his wife. This tradition came to us from the West.

Those of us enamoured in following [the West] and its people in everything believe that they do not possess [the ability] to divorce their wives.[76] And we have heard so much about their opposition to divorce in Islam, that we have prohibited it for ourselves! All while the Europeans and Americans are beginning to make it easier for themselves.[77] They have taken ease from us, while we have taken restrictions from them.

So, the one who grows weary of his partner such that he feels the need to replace her through immorality [i.e. through fornication] would be able to benefit from the power [of divorce] to exchange one wife for another, which is in his grasp. He may find in Islam a reprieve from falling into the prohibited, or even plunging into the havoc of polygamy altogether.[78] Who knows? Perhaps he can find happiness in his second marriage, and his old wife, who becomes new for the one who marries her after him, can find

---

[76] Divorce is strictly forbidden for members of the Roman Catholic Church, although not for members of most Protestant churches. Even still, in Protestant-majority Western countries such as the United Kingdom or the United States in the 1930s, divorce was difficult to obtain. An Act of Parliament in 1937 in the United Kingdom, for example, expanded grounds for divorce to include cruelty, desertion and incurable insanity; prior to this, divorce could only be obtained on grounds of adultery, and before the Matrimonial Causes Act of 1923, only men could petition for divorce in cases of adultery. See: UK Parliament, "Divorce since 1900" https://www.parliament.uk/business/publications/research/olympic-britain/housing-and-home-life/split-pairs/. Last accessed 27 November, 2023.

[77] Divorce slowly became normalised in Western countries over the course of the 20th century, parallel with a broad decline in religiosity. According to the statistical office of the European Union, Eurostat, 60% of births in France occurred out of wedlock in 2016. The same was true for more than 50% of births in Sweden, Denmark, Portugal and the Netherlands in the same year. See: "Are More Babies Born inside or Outside Marriage?" Are More Babies Born inside or Outside Marriage? - Products Eurostat News - Eurostat, ec.europa.eu/eurostat/web/products-eurostat-news/-/ddn-20180416-1. Accessed 30 Nov. 2023.

[78] That is, a sexually-unsatisfied man who divorces and remarries may become so satisfied with his new wife that he need not take on the burden of becoming polygamous.

happiness as well.[79]

On Complicating Marriage through Raising the Marriage Age

Maintaining chastity [among the youth] is helped chiefly by not making the process of marriage difficult by stipulating for it a specific age, or by delaying marriage years beyond the puberty of both sexes. Who can [seriously] guarantee that young boys and girls can pass through these long years, the flowering of their youth and the boiling of their blood, and spend them in chastity and [religious] devotion?! The fact that they are too busy with studies for marriage at this stage of life is no excuse for their parents to take so little concern for their physical needs. Nor is it an excuse for the youth themselves, because they are considered legally mature and accountable. No one has ever been given a licence to be corrupt on the basis that he is a student and it is impossible for him to marry.

The law of Islam obligates marriage for everyone who fears himself susceptible to corruption, and does not allow for anyone to fall into fornication even if they are in their stages of study. Rather, Muslims are obliged to devise a way to harmonise learning with marriage in order to protect the chastity of students.[80]

And human nature (*fiṭra*) does not permit the stage of fervent youth to pass by in inactivity and waste, nor [does it permit] reproduction in an improper way, ultimately leading to waste [once more].

And yet, because we saw that Westerners do not marry in the vigour of their youth, we started blindly following them. We never considered that they do not care if their youth serve their physical needs in

---

[79] Meaning, perhaps divorcees will find happiness with their new spouses. This notion is borrowed from the Qur'ānic exhortation that, "But if they choose to separate, Allah will enrich both from His bounties. And Allah is Ever-Bountiful, All-Wise." [*al-Nisā'*: 130]

[80] According to the findings of several research papers published in 2014 by the Family and Youth Institute, nearly 54% of American Muslim college students report having engaged in premarital sex, while a broader age sample yielded that nearly 67% of US & Canadian Muslims have engaged in the same. Of the remaining who had not, perhaps more religiously inclined, nearly 50% had considered doing so at one point or another, while many others have sought refuge in secret marriages as an alternative, citing it being the lesser of two evils (*akhaff al-ḍararayn*). While less than the reported 90% average among the broader American student population engaging in premarital sex, this statistic is still quite alarming. With rampant premarital sex and growing rates of secret marriages that present another set of unique problems, the need for open conversation and viable solutions such as family-supported marriages for students, as suggested by Ṣabrī nearly a century ago, needs to be adequately considered and applied. Furthermore, Ṣabrī's suggestion–rendering this issue one of communal obligation in the legal religious sense–is perhaps more justified now than ever before. See: "Pre-Marital Sex among Muslim Youth." The Family and Youth Institute, 30 Jan. 2023, www.thefyi.org/infographics/pre-marital-sex-among-muslim-youth/

ways unacceptable to Islamic social ethics, such as mixing with, embracing, and exchanging [expressions of] love with young women. Or [worse,] perhaps we did consider this, and yet followed them with indifference [all the same].

Retaining with Honour or Separating with Grace

In brief: Islam is easy. It wishes for us ease in our affairs, and its scheme with regards to husbands and their wives revolves around either keeping them with kindness, or leaving them with goodness, as mentioned in the Qur'ān.[81]

And although marriage is, naturally, a firm commitment as expressed in the Qur'ān,[82] with divorce being most hated of that which Allāh permits,[83] along with [the fact that] Allāh loves not the 'samplers', as mentioned in the Prophetic narration;[84] nothing from these [textual injunctions] joins one spouse to the other such that they cannot separate, as [was the case] in the marriages of all previous nations.

[In Islām], the man holds [the power of] divorce (*ṭalāq*) and so does the woman if *she* stipulates it in the marriage contract,[85] or through the

---

[81] "Divorce may be retracted twice, then the husband must retain his wife with honour or separate from her with grace..." [*al-Baqara*: 229]

[82] "And how could you take it back after having enjoyed each other intimately and she has taken from you a firm commitment?" [*al-Nisā'*: 21]

[83] It was narrated by 'Abd Allāh b. 'Umar (may Allāh be pleased with him) that the Prophet (ﷺ) said, "Of all the lawful acts the most detestable to Allāh is divorce." *Sunan Abū Dāwūd* (2173) Chapter: The Disliked Nature of Divorce.

[84] This is in reference to the statement of the Prophet (ﷺ) that, "do not divorce women except with suspicion [meaning, a legitimate reason]; certainly, Allāh–glory be to Him–does not love the male or female samplers." Explaining the narration, al-Munāwī (d. 1031/1621) states that "[the samplers are those who] marry with the goal of sexual gratification (*dhawq al-'usayla*), and once that is achieved, they separate. Marriage for this reason is severely disliked as is divorce without suspicion; meaning, without a valid reason." See: al-Munāwī, Muḥammad 'Abd al-Ra'ūf. 1972. *Fayḍ al-Qadīr Sharḥ al-Jāmi' al-Saghīr*. Vol. 6, 6 Vols. Beirut: Dār al-Ma'rifa li 'l-Tibā'a wa 'l-Nashr. 411. For the narration, see: *al-Bazzār* (8/70), and al-Ṭabarānī, *al-Mu'jam al-Awsaṭ* (8/24).

[85] It is important to note that this is an issue of disagreement (*ikhtilāf*) between the scholars of the four Sunni schools. The majority of scholars held such a clause to invalidate the contract. The Shāfi'ī and Ḥanbalī schools held the contract to be rendered void at the mere stipulation of such a clause. The Mālikī school held that the contract must be invalidated, however, if the marriage had been consummated before the dissolution, the marriage would remain valid but the condition would be terminated. The Ḥanafī school (with which Ṣabrī was affiliated), however, held exception, permitting such a stipulation when verbalised by the woman during the marriage contract, as opposed to the man. The right to entrust divorce (*tafwīḍ al-ṭalāq*) to the woman, while permitted among the majority of scholars during the marriage, would be invalid outside marriage. As such, if the man raised the stipulation during the marriage contract, the woman would be accepting a right he does not yet possess, and this would then be rendered void. In the opposite case, however, if the woman proposes this clause, the man would be accepting the marriage with a right he, subsequent to the agreed marriage proposal, possesses and can relinquish at any point, making it within the confines of the marriage

khul'.[86] It can also be held by two adjudicators from their families, sent to rectify their affairs [in cases of conflict].[87] [This is] because the continuation of the marriage bond, even though it is sought in Islam and cherished, is contingent upon the couple not fearing to breach the boundaries of Allāh. This is also the expression of the Qur'ān.[88] [The exegetes] explain these [boundaries] as referring to women's marital rights [from their husbands] which are similar to their responsibilities [to their husbands] in that both maintain goodness, while also entailing a rank for men above them.[89] And

---

itself, and hence valid. For more on *tafwīḍ al-ṭalāq*, see: Khan, Fareeha. "*Traditionalist Approaches to Sharī'ah Reform: Mawlana Ashraf 'Ali Thānawi's Fatwa on Women's Right to Divorce.*" Doctoral thesis, University of Michigan, 2008, 133ff.

[86] There are several ways in Islam through which a marriage can be dissolved. These include *ṭalāq* (divorce), *faskh* (annulment), and the *khul'*. The *khul'* is a process through which a woman may obtain separation from her husband in return for a payment. The husband, who might otherwise not be willing to give a divorce out of his own volition (seeing that he has monetarily invested into the relationship through the bridal dowry (*mahr*), could be motivated to do so through this payment, which would usually amount to the dowry amount, but could be greater or less as well. This type of separation is supported by the Qur'ānic injunction, "...So if you fear they will not be able to keep within the limits of Allāh, there is no blame if the wife compensates the husband to obtain a divorce." Qur'ān 2:229, as well as the narration of Thābit b. Qays (may Allāh be pleased with him) whose wife obtained a divorce from him after he accepted the Prophet's (ﷺ) suggestion that she surrender the garden he had given her in dowry before the marriage. See: *Ṣaḥīḥ al-Bukhārī* (5273) Chapter: A *Khul'* and How Divorce is Given According to It.

[87] "If you anticipate a split between them, appoint a mediator from his family and another from hers. If they desire reconciliation, Allah will restore harmony between them. Surely Allah is All-Knowing, All-Aware." [*al-Nisā'*: 35]

[88] "...It is not lawful for husbands to take back anything of the dowry given to their wives, unless the couple fears not being able to keep within the limits of Allah. So if you fear they will not be able to keep within the limits of Allah, there is no blame if the wife compensates the husband to obtain divorce. These are the limits set by Allah, so do not transgress them..." [*al-Baqara*: 229]

[89] "...Women have rights similar to those of men equitably, although men have a degree above them..." [*al-Baqara*: 228] Classical and contemporary exegetes (*mufassirūn*) of the Qur'ān have provided numerous explanations for what men having a degree over women entails. Classical authorities tend to cite that this degree for men over women refers to their rights, or to their virtue. The former because while women possess rights to the bridal dowry, maintenance, and not being harmed, men additionally possess the rights to the women themselves, as well as divorce, and its revoking. As far as virtue is concerned, while both share in the duties of sexual intimacy, men also hold greater responsibilities in providing for the women, and in their maintenance. Most scholars cite the Qur'ānic verse "Men are the caretakers of women, as men have been provisioned by Allah over women and tasked with supporting them financially..." [*al-Nisā'*: 34] as proof for this. This provisionment and bestowal from Allāh over women has commonly held to refer to their greater physical strength, and their overall greater intellect (though this latter idea is contended by more contemporary reformist writers). Some scholars have also cited these two verses in reference to the domestic duties of the wife, one in which men are supposed to assist, while duties outside the home are primarily allocated to men. These scholars also root this ideal familial framework in the Prophetic guidelines laid out for his daughter Fāṭima with her husband 'Alī (may Allāh be pleased with them both). He tasked her with domestic duties while 'Alī would be responsible for working outside the home, and taking the duties of leadership within the city in the Prophet's (ﷺ) absence. The longest discussion on this topic can be found in Ibn 'Āshūr's explanation of the verse. See: Ibn 'Āshūr, Ṭāhir. *al-Taḥrīr wa 'l-Tanwīr*. Vol. 2. 30 vols. Tunis: al-Dār al-Tūnīsiyya li 'l-Nashr, 1984, 2/396-403.

this manner of expression exalts those rights in a way that cannot be concealed.

Additionally, it is not hidden that protecting the chastity of both parties is one of the objectives set out in establishing the boundaries (*ḥudūd*) of Allāh first and foremost. So if a breaching of Allāh's boundaries is feared from the disobedience of one, then divorce is prescribed with softness, kindness, and goodness. It makes no sense for them to spend their lives unhappy [with each other and the relationship], and it is a transgression of the limits of Allāh on the part of the woman for her to deny her husband polygamy, which is his right, should he need it.

The Islamic Balance: Between Christian Rigidity & Socialist Chaos

In this freedom to marry or divorce, and the ease with which the two spouses navigate it, Islam strikes a balance between the essential distinction of the Christians [i.e. exclusivism in marriage] and the chaos of the socialists.[90] [The Islamic model] is not far in its essence from socialism (*ishtirāk*), and guarantees benefits for mankind expected [from socialism], while freeing it from extremes. And the *zakāt* of Islam which sees a claim for the poor in the wealth of the rich, is a testament to this.

Likewise, the ease of marriage and divorce in Islam, including the ease of replacing one spouse with another, is of this type, meaning: it is one way in which Islam resembles socialism. It is with this ease that Islam can recognize [some] people's need to reinvigorate [their married life], which reprobates and socialists have made absolute.[91] Islam offers renewal within boundaries and binds it to an organised system.

The *Anṣār* of Medina used to support the *Muhājirīn* among the Companions of the Prophet (may Allāh be pleased with them all),[92] to the

---

[90] It was commonly held by socialists and communists in the early 20th century, such as in the newly established USSR, that traditional marriage bonds were relics of an outdated social system. The 1918 Soviet "Code on Marriage, the Family and Guardianship" introduced "no-grounds" divorces, and abolished the concept of illegitimate birth, among other changes. The USSR later reverted to a more conservative family code in 1926. See: Goldman, Wendy. *Women, the State, and Revolution: Soviet Family Policy and Social Life, 1917-1936*. Cambridge: Cambridge University Press, 1993.

[91] Ṣabrī is criticising both Christians and socialists for dealing in absolutes. They either forbid divorce altogether, or attach no commitment to marriage whatsoever, in his view. Islam, he suggests, is the middle path.

[92] The *Muhājirīn* (Migrants) were the early Muslims of Mecca who followed the Prophet to Medina to escape persecution by the pagan rulers of their home city. The *Anṣār* (Disciples) were the Muslim converts of Medina who received the Prophet and the *Muhājirīn*, and helped them settle in their new home. The Prophet famously paired off Medinese and Meccan Muslims to help one another as brothers, and bring together the two parts of the Muslim community in a spirit of brotherhood.

extent that an *Anṣārī* who had two wives would separate from one, and marry her off to one of them [i.e. the *Muhājirīn*].[93] This is [but] one proof for the ease of marriage and divorce in Islam, and that the object of both is selflessness and sacrifice, not selfishness and monopolisation.[94]

Polygamy within Divine Law, and Polyamory Outside Marriage

We return to polygamy, and compare it to having multiple partners outside of marriage–something preferred by those entirely engorged by the mindset of blindly imitating those foreign to Islam with its legislation of polygamy–and they [falsely] attribute this preference to [all] women.

I have spoken about this comparison in my aforementioned book: "In the unregulated taking of multiple partners lies:

- harm to the husband who loses his chastity;
- harm to the [second] woman with whom he conjugates, who loses her chastity, and
- harm to the wife insofar as she is married to a man who has lost his chastity.
- It also harms her as she may possibly lose her chastity in seeking revenge upon her husband, and it is [in turn]
- harmful to the husband in this respect. It is also
- harmful to the husband of the woman with whom he conjugates if she is married. Further, it is
- harmful for the wife of the husband with whom the first wife conjugates out of revenge against her own husband, and it is
- harmful for the children who are lost between all these fornicators. It is also
- harmful for all involved due to transmittable diseases which may arise from all these conjugations, and [finally,] it is

[93] The only reported incidence of this was when the Companion Sa'd b. al-Rabī', an *Anṣārī*, offered to divorce one of his two wives for the *Muhājir* 'Abd al-Raḥmān b. 'Awf. The latter politely declined, saying "May God bless you and your family, your property; please tell me where the market is." *Ṣaḥīḥ al-Bukhārī* (3781) Chapter: Merits of the Helpers in Medina.

[94] "...They give the emigrants preference over themselves even though they may be in need. And whoever is saved from the selfishness of their own souls, it is they who are truly successful." [*al-Ḥashr*: 9]

- harmful for the wives of these conjugators, and the husbands of the conjugating women who spread diseases through their fornication.

These are ten harms, the last three of which lead to immediate harm in one's life.[95]

And Allāh has wisely willed that debilitating [sexually-transmitted] diseases should take hold as a result of these unlegislated conjugations.

And polygamy, in comparison to these ten, contains [just] one [*supposed*] harm limited only to the wife, i.e. that her husband marries another woman, which, even if it is a harm insofar as it does not leave her husband to her exclusively, at least does not remove her honour. Her husband has simply exercised his Islamic right. The [wife's] situation is analogous to the birth of a younger brother after a son, who thereby no longer had a monopoly on his parents' attention."[96]

I am not someone who does not attach value to love and the heart, and the bond between them that gives life or death. Nor am I someone who does not appreciate those compassionate husbands who, out of love for their spouses, or at the least out of mercy, do not marry someone else, even if they need it. The Prophet (ﷺ) said, "Whoever is gentle with my Ummah, Allāh is gentle with him."[97]

I truly do not understand those writers in opposition [to polygamy], those who put on such a display of care and value for the heart and love of the first wife, all while easily pardoning the betrayal she and her love face from a husband who cheats with another woman, instead of marrying her. This is despite the fact that the attack against the heart in the first case [of him having an affair] is worse and uglier [than polygamy] because sharing in that [illegitimate] love includes the downfall of everyone involved.[98]

Polygamy's Burden for One Woman

---

[95] All ten issues raised by Ṣabrī are harmful, but the first seven are primarily harms to one's morality, heart, and character, and their effects may not be fully felt until Judgment Day, if one were able to hide their infidelity until death, for example. The last three, by contrast, will undoubtedly cause immediate problems in one's worldly life.

[96] See: Ṣabrī. *Dini Müceddidler* (Reformers of the Religion), 332. See: Ṣabrī (n. 70), at 40.

[97] The narration above can be found as an authentically reported Prophetic supplication in *Musnad Aḥmad* (40/393): "May Allāh be gentle with those who are gentle with my Ummah." See: Ṣabrī (n. 70), at 42 fn.1.

[98] The dignity of all parties; the cheating husband, his wife, and his mistress, is compromised in the case of him having an extramarital affair. On the other hand, in the case that he takes a second wife, everyone retains their dignity.

Contains Benefit for Another Like Her

Polygamy, even if it is tough on the first wife and hurts her, still benefits another of her sex–making her a wife like the first, as opposed to a lowly girlfriend.

And humanity, if it looked to polygamy, and its contrast of taking multiple partners without regulation–which must necessarily fill the void left by legislated polygamy–if humanity considered both without bias, it would find that [legislated] polygamy is more beneficial to women in general, and in improving their overall state. Meanwhile, the opponent looks [only] to the benefit of some [women,] at the expense of others.

Let alone that, if [it is alleged that] polygamy deprives the sexes of equality, [it must be acknowledged that] man is not equal to woman. Polygamy speaks to a lack of equality; the human nature (*fiṭra*) of a woman which refuses to engage in polyandry in response to polygamy, as we have mentioned, itself speaks to that lack of equality.

Furthermore, a woman is unable to give birth more than once in a year, whereas man's reproductive power renews every day, and nothing can prevent him [from fathering children]. Furthermore, a woman is not in need of a man during the days of her menstruation, postpartum bleeding, and childbirth. She also becomes an old woman before the man, at which point she is unable to give birth; [physical] oldness strikes her before she becomes old [in years]. So she is a virgin, then a married woman (*thayyib*), then a mother, and her [physical] tenderness and freshness pass away through each stage. If we were to restrict men and women in the balance of equality–so as to be just to women–we would oppress the man who is superior in his natural composition.[99]

---

[99] This prescient warning from Ṣabrī has all but proven true in the modern world. Systems designed to accommodate both males and females often hinder the development and needs of one or the other. Many have remarked that modern public education systems, for example, are considerably feminised and place boys at a disadvantage against female peers, whose brains develop earlier. While solutions such as 'redshirting' may mitigate the problem, they fail to address the root cause underlying this crisis. The entire system of education, on which later success in adult life is almost always predicated in modern times, is designed around this equality legislation and norms. They may assist girls in the short-term, but by ignoring the needs of both genders, often prove destructive to boys (and subsequently, the women around them) in the long-term. See: Reeves, Richard V. "Redshirt the Boys: Why Boys Should Start School a Year Later than Girls." *The Atlantic*, October 2022. https://www.theatlantic.com/magazine/archive/2022/10/boys-delayed-entry-school-start-redshirting/671238/. Last Accessed: December 1st, 2023.

Is it not noticeable that even a mother prefers her child to be male? Does this not indicate recognition by the woman of man's superiority?[100]

The claim of "equality between men and women" began to spread in modern times under the patronage of some men advocating on behalf of women–because of an internal need within themselves. They attempt to take care [of their needs] with them by drawing close to them.[101] So if the cause of [such alleged] equality succeeds, the woman is successful in gaining an equality that is only *granted* and not authentic.[102]

Women in our era try to compete with men by raising the heels of their shoes; a competition predicated on pretensions and changing [their] natural disposition. However, they should beware that [it may be those very same] heels that puts them in danger of tripping in this race with men.

Increasing Reproduction Among Nations & the Unreasonable Contentions of Cenab Şehabeddin Bey

Given what we have mentioned regarding the superiority of men's reproductive capabilities, such that even a large group of women cannot compare to even a single man, the way to increase progeny among nations, in light of this, is to marry one man to a number of women. And this Islamic fundamental is something Western governments will need to establish in their lands, especially after one of them does so.[103]

As for having much progeny, there is no doubt that it is one of the most venerated means by which nations seek power. No one doubts its benefits, except a writer who once wrote in *al-Ahrām*[104] prohibiting

---

[100] Şabrī discusses the issue of equality between men and women in greater detail later in the book. See pages: 119-123.

[101] Şabrī here describes the case of some male feminists, who champion women's causes out of a conscious or subconscious desire to gain the approval and intimacy of women around them, i.e. to acquire romantic partners. In the case of conscious efforts placed forward, this would be considered predatory behaviour.

[102] Şabrī correctly points out that there would be no legal or social equality between men and women were it not for men freely granting women that equality, in Western nations in the early and mid-20th century, and most Muslim nations some decades later.

[103] Şabrī suggests that in seeking to increase their populations, Western nations will one day need to allow polygamy. Although it is unlikely that he foresaw the major decline in fertility which took place across the Western world over the 20th and 21st centuries, it has nonetheless become a major policy issue. According to UN estimates, the average number of children per woman in Europe has declined from 2.7 in 1950 to 1.49 in 2022. See: Statista Research Department. "Total Fertility Rate in Europe from 1950 to 2022." Statista, February 28, 2023. Last Accessed: December, 14th, 2023. https://www.statista.com/statistics/1251565/total-fertility-rate-in-europe.

[104] *Al-Ahrām* ("The Pyramids") is one of the oldest and most reputable newspapers in the Arabic language. It

Egyptians from having many children. All the while, Western governments are competing to increase the number of their citizens. In fact, they are remunerating those with many children; offering various benefits to them, just as our Prophet (ﷺ) said before, "marry and multiply; for I will boast of your great numbers before the nations on the Day of Judgment."[105]

And I was surprised by the perversity of this writer who, we praise Allāh, did not meddle in the debate on polygamy. If he had, he would have [surely] considered the fact that polygamy serves to increase progeny to be a harmful effect.

Even stranger was what a major writer in Turkey[106] mentioned previously, when I debated him on the issue of polygamy; that he did not consider the increasing of life to be from its benefits. I mention him here that he may be an example of the opposition's arrogance in this issue, and a proof for the feebleness of their footing–to the point that they must often reinforce their claims with that which contradicts basic intuition and common sense.

Furthermore, it is men who take up life's harshest jobs. Women of recent generations sharing with them in some small portion of it is the furthest thing from true equality. It should be sufficient for you that the essential burdens of war lie on the shoulders [of men]; the blood flowing in these wars like rivers is theirs.[107]

As such, nations need their women to take up sacrifice commensurate with a portion of what men sacrifice, and suffer the loss these sacrifices entail. These women should wage war on themselves, and bear with acceptance the burden of polygamy. In carrying this heavy burden, they will be compensated in kind for men's sacrifice of their souls on the battlefield.

---

was founded in Alexandria in 1875 by two Lebanese Christians, and has since been a fixture in Egyptian society, and the Arab world.

[105] See: 'Abd al-Razzāq. *Al-Muṣannaf* (6/173). Other narrations to this meaning also include, "Marry those who are loving and fertile, for I will boast of your great numbers before the nations." *Sunan Abū Dāwūd* (2050) Chapter: The Prohibition Of Marrying Women Who Do Not Give Birth. See: See: Ṣabrī (n. 70), at 44 fn.1.

[106] [Muṣṭafā Ṣabrī]: "Cenab Şehabeddin Bey (d. 1934), may Allāh have mercy on him." Cenab, son of Osman Şehâbeddîn, was a prolific Ottoman and later Turkish physician, poet, and literateur. He studied at the Gülhane Military Medical Academy in Istanbul before travelling to France for a number of years for specialisation in his field. His residency in France allowed him to study French literature, to which he took a great liking. After returning to Istanbul, he continued working as a physician at the Haydarpaşa hospital, and began to write prose and poetry for *al-Maktab* newspaper. Born around the same time as Ṣabrī, he passed away earlier at the age of 62 in Istanbul on February 12th, 1934.

[107] It is worth noting that *Qawlī fī al-Mar'a* was written in the 1930s, with the memory of the First World War, the deadliest conflict in human history to that point, fresh in the public consciousness.

And the opposing writer's statement, which we have previously noted, "if war was to occur and a large number of men died, it would then be possible for us to return to our religion, and to apply [polygamy] based on changing times," is recognition from him of the roots of polygamy. He recognises that it is a right of men in the context of wars; he expresses as much without realising it, and without knowing that postponement [of polygamy] does not harmonise with that recognized benefit. [This is] because the fruits of polygamy established in wake of a war, and the death of a large number of men, come only decades after the end of that war.

The matter at hand: a vigilant *Ummah* is obliged to remain, after one war has ended, capable of fighting another. So, it is necessary for it to always be prepared, and not wait until the hour of need.[108]

Twenty-five years ago in Turkey, I wrote that polygamy, which is a burden carried by women, is comparable to the wars of men. I later came across a Prophetic narration and wrote it in my aforementioned book,[109] and that is, "Allāh has prescribed jealousy (*ghayra*) upon women,[110] and *jihād* upon men. And whosoever is patient with them, with conviction [that it is from Allah], and seeks [their] reward from Allāh, [s]he will have a reward like that of the martyr." [This is] narrated by al-Ṭabarānī (d. 360/918)[111] from Ibn Mas'ūd, with an acceptable chain, *al-Jāmi' al-Ṣaghīr*.[112] There is an indication towards polygamy in the narration.[113]

---

[108] Essentially, one cannot prepare for a circumstance after it becomes a reality. If polygamy is the solution for the negative consequences of war and a form of preparation for future wars, it must exist before any such future war. This circular paradigm thus brings about the perpetual, innate need for a polygamous society. This need finds further support in the Islamic legal principle that any prerequisite to the performance of an obligatory (*wājib*) act consequently becomes obligatory itself. See: Āl-Borno, Muḥammad. *al-Wajīz fī Īḍāḥ Qawā'id al-Fiqh al-Kulliya*. Beirut, Lebanon: al-Mu'assasat al-Risāla al-'Ālamiyya, 393.

[109] *Dini Müceddidler* (Reformers of the Religion), 322. See: Ṣabrī (n. 70), at 45.

[110] *Ghayra*, as described earlier, is a form of protective, righteous jealousy enjoined upon Muslims. This is distinct from covetous jealousy (*ḥasad*), which is to be condemned. To have *ghayra* is to be jealous of one's spouse, for example, i.e. to not want anyone else of the opposite sex to spend time with them, or to jealously protect their honour. This exists for women as it does for men, though it is less heightened. The wives of the Prophet (ﷺ) would often mention the jealousy they felt over him. Umm Salama expressed herself as a jealous woman upon his proposal, and 'Ā'isha would remark that she never felt jealous of any of the wives of the Prophet (ﷺ) like she did over his first wife, Khadīja (may Allāh be pleased with them all). See: *Sunan al-Nasa'ī* (3254) Chapter: A Son Conducting the Marriage for His Mother, *Ṣaḥīḥ al-Bukhārī* (3818) Chapter: The Marriage of the Prophet (ﷺ) with Khadija (may Allāh be pleased with her) and Her Superiority.

[111] The authenticity of this narration is questioned by Ḥadīth scholars as it contains 'Ubayd b. al-Ṣabbāḥ (d. 235/849) upon whose reliability there is dispute. See: al-Ṭabarānī, Abū 'l-Qāsim. *al-Mu'jam al-Kabīr* 10/87., al-Bazzār, Abū Bakr. *Musnad al-Bazzār* 4/308. See: Ṣabrī (n. 70), at 46 fn.1.

[112] See: al-Munāwī, 'Abd al-Ra'ūf. *Fayḍ al-Qadīr* 2/249. See: Ṣabrī (n. 70), at 46 fn.2.

[113] This narration is indicating that women, who possess protective jealousy similar to men, are nonetheless tasked with needing to have patience if their husband procures other wives. This same patience is not asked of men who possess exclusive rights over their wives, but are otherwise tasked with fighting in the path of

And what is intended by the prescription of jealousy in women is the prescription of what would cause that jealousy–which is polygamy. We have explained this because jealousy is also found in men, but they are not charged with it, i.e. that which causes it, like women have been charged.

[With that], we should conclude this article, as it has become drawn-out for the reader...

In summary: in polygamy lies certain safety and protection from sexual vice, and power for the nation that practises it.

Allāh and maintaining patience over risking their lives. The Prophet (ﷺ) is indicating that the reward of such women who have to tolerate their husbands seeking other wives or those in polygamous relationships is similar to the great reward bestowed upon the martyr who fights in the path of Allāh, and ultimately gives his life for that cause.

ON UNVEILING AND VEILING

There is no dispute that the [Near] East is the cradle of civilisations and knowledge. This is because it is the homeland of prophets and the place where divine revelation was sent down. Even the Greek civilisation, which is the oldest in Europe, and that by which the West was illuminated before its illumination with the knowledge of Islam–when its civilisation which was established in Spain at the hands of the conquering Arabs–itself borrowed from its connection with the inhabitants of the Asiatic coasts by trade and other means, not to mention the original Greeks themselves being migrants from the East.

Unveiling is Primitive, while Veiling Indicates Religious & Moral Development

There is also no dispute that unveiling (*al-sufūr*) reflects a primitive, primordial state of man, or that veiling (*al-iḥtijāb*) arose after mankind's development of religious and moral conscience which inhibits [men] from chaos in natural, physical circumstances. [Veiling] prevents the means [by which chaos takes hold], and acts as a barrier between males and females.

And veiling was made specific to the woman as opposed to the man, because he is busy outside the house, and because his position in sexual circumstances is that of a pursuer, and the position of the woman is that which is being pursued, so he seeks and asserts, and she accepts or rejects.

Her veiling is a medal of her rejection, with which she is decorated in front of the man, so that he need not be rejected and turned away by tongue or by hand. And in it lies her security from being the object of man's desire.

So if a man approaches her or tries to seduce her with his eyes, and if she wants to accept his advances, she lifts her veil for him, and he understands that she has accepted his pursuit. Furthermore, her unveiling for a specific man without his pursuit is a sign that she would accept his pursuit, and lures him into seeking her. Her general unveiling is a symbol of general acceptance and enticement.

Veiling Compliments Natural Ghayra, while Desires Delude into Unveiling

So veiling, while it restricts against the general chaos of natural sexual circumstances–and in this respect contradicts nature, is [also] harmonious with the protective jealousy (*al-ghayra*) with which humans have been created and agrees with nature from another angle. Protective jealousy, however, is an instinct whose power extends from the soul, while unrestricted freedom in sexual circumstances [is an impulse which arises] from [physical] sexual desires. So this [chaos] is enticed by unveiling, and that [jealousy] is [served] by covering, and between these two instincts, a war rages inside man.

Western civilisation has chosen the first side (i.e. that of sexual desires) and decided not to prohibit its people from enjoying the sweetness of unveiled women, and the mixing of the sexes in clubs and late-night soirées. It sacrifices the second natural state in pursuit of that enjoyment.

As a result, the Western man mixes with all women, kissing their hands, sitting with them while they are exposed and half-naked, and he embraces them, thus conceding his protective jealousy over his wife, sister, and daughter, as other men mix with, sit among, and embrace his women. As he sees it, the cost is small in comparison to what he reaps in profit; perhaps he does not even possess anyone to sacrifice, so he simply enjoys pure profit.

These soirées, essential concomitants (*lawāzim*) of a civilised society in the West, are nothing but a pronounced, open support for that mixed society and seeking to draw one sex closer to the other in conjugation and bondage. It also kills protective jealousy within those from whom it is most expected, and in whose best interests it lies. It is as if those parties were mere open orgies.

Suspending Ghayra Contradicts Nature & Virtue

The elimination of protective jealousy in Western civilisation reached such a degree that it began to be considered a defect, while a human being would [naturally] judge it a virtue. Its writers and its poets were ashamed to change this natural inclination; as the famous French poet

[Victor] Hugo (d. 1885)[114] wrote to the International Peace Congress in Lugano [Switzerland] in the year 1872:[115]

> "We shall have the spirit of conquest transfigured into the spirit of discovery; we shall have the generous fraternity of nations in place of the ferocious fraternity of emperors; our country will be without frontiers, our budget without parasitism, our travel without barrier, education without brutality, our commerce without duties, youth without barracks, courage without combat, our justice without the scaffold, life without murder, [the forest without the tiger, the plough without the sword,] speech without censure, conscience without judgement, truth without dogma, God without the priest, heaven without hell, and passionate love without hostility and exploitation [Hugo: love without hate]. [The dreadful binding of civilisation will be defeated; the terrible isthmus which separates the seas of mankind and felicity will be cut. There shall be on earth a flow of light. And what is all this light? It is liberty. And what is all this liberty? It is peace.]"[116]

And by 'passionate love without hostility and exploitation' he [Hugo] meant that liberal expansiveness will replace the strictness of protective jealousy.

The Advice of the French Poetess to Eastern Women

And despite this, people of clean nature in the West feel the bitterness of this mixed society, and speak with sadness of this grave truth;

---

[114] Victor Hugo (d. 1885) was, aside from a novelist, a French Senator and Member of the National Assembly. He was one of the most influential liberal thinkers of France in the 19th century. He showed considerable interest in Islam and wrote sympathetically toward the religion, leading some to speculate that he may have privately held Muslim beliefs, though this has not been proven definitively. He had mixed feelings about imperialism; in his most famous novel, *Les Misérables,* he condemned the French colonisation of Algeria: "Algeria was too harshly conquered, and, as in the case of India by the English, with more barbarism than civilisation." See: Hugo, Victor. *Les Misérables,* Random House Publishing, 2000, 720.

[115] Hugo was a longtime member of the International Peace Congress, presiding over the 1849 session in Paris, where he first delivered a speech similar in content to that quoted here by Ṣabrī. His speech written for the 1872 session in Lugano, titled "My European Compatriots" promised a bright future for Europe and for mankind. Hugo did not actually attend this session in-person, as he was occupied in the English Channel island of Guernsey.

[116] This section from Hugo has been translated directly from the original French. Ṣabrī's rendering of the speech is slightly different than the original, with several omissions and imprecise ordering of some predictions; these have been included here in brackets. See: Hugo, Victor. "L'Avenir de l'Europe." In *Actes et Paroles*, Vol. III. Paris: J. Hetzel, 1880. https://www.atramenta.net/lire/oeuvre5715-chapitre-53.html.

so has written the greatest Turkish writer, Cenab Şehabeddin Bey,[117] in his book titled *Evrak-ı Eyyam* about Madame Delarue-Mardrus (d. 1945),[118] whom he describes as one of the greatest poets of France. She said to him:

> "Tell your women to appreciate their own happiness, and how the compulsion of a veiled life protects them from so many sources of unease. Do they not know the number of women beloved to me who cry piled upon my shoulder?! Lodged in my ears are gut-wrenching complaints from women, oh yes! Entering these grand dance parties is seen as a fitting invitation for [men to] pursue [a woman romantically], however the protective jealousy which bites at a wife's heart enters these parties along with her dearly beloved husband. It is like a venomous viper,[119] oh what a snake! Do you know that? The dance parties, theatres, and meeting halls; they are nothing but [memories] of the *Sainte Office*'s [Holy Office of the Catholic Church] torture chambers,[120] and nothing but hell before the man concerned with his wife's affairs, or a woman who loves

---

[117] Cenab Şehabeddin Bey advocated for reforms in Islamic law and Ottoman society; one article in particular, "Yarinki Efkar-ı İslamiyye" (*Peyâm-ı Sabah*, 13 Kânunusâni, 1337) in which he argued against the necessity of veiling for women, and complained of Islam's lack of appreciation for fine arts such as sculpture, attracted harsh criticism from Muṣṭafā Ṣabrī and İskilipi Atıf Hoca. In another article titled "Hâtime-i Münazara" (*Peyâm-ı Sabah*, 17 Kânunusâni, 1337) he argued that despite the complaints of some 'ulamā', some *ijtihād* must be done in favour of accommodating modern necessities. Ṣabrī, in a religious newspaper (*Alemdar*, 19 Kânunusâni 1337), said that overturning the religious law was beyond both his, and Şehabeddin's authority. Despite disagreements, however, Ṣabrī nevertheless greatly respected Şehabeddin Bey, referring to him here as "the greatest Turkish writer". It may be gathered that he was not one of the extreme advocates of Westernisation who Ṣabrī devotes much of this book to refuting. See: Tarakçı, Celal. "Cenab Şahabeddin (1871–1934)." In *TDV İslâm Ansiklopedisi*, Vol. 7. Istanbul: TDV İslâm Araştırmaları Merkezi, 1993. Last Accessed: December 15th, 2023. https://islamansiklopedisi.org.tr/cenab-sahabeddin.

[118] Lucie Delarue-Mardrus was a French poet, novelist and artist. She authored more than 70 books in her lifetime, some of which became quite popular. She was a highly independent and eccentric woman; although once married to a French-Arabic translator, she divorced him and devoted her life completely to her artistic pursuits and social life. She was an open lesbian and wrote extensively on women's sexuality. She had some experience with the Muslim world, travelling to Morocco and Tunisia in 1905. See: Albert-Sorel, André. *Lucie Delarue-Mardrus, sirène de l'Estuaire, née-native de Honfleur.* 1999. Éd. de la Lieutenance, Honfleur.

[119] Ṣabrī is referring here to a specific viper species native to West Asia, called the Eirenis viper.

[120] This is a reference to the Holy Office of the Inquisition, a mediaeval Catholic institution which sought out and punished heretics. The Inquisition is most famous for its activities in Spain, where among others, Andalusian Muslims from lands conquered by the Spanish Crown were tortured, killed and forced to convert to Catholicism. Delarue-Mardrus here is compares modern dance parties, theatres, and meeting halls to the mediaeval torture chambers of the Inquisition for the jealous feelings they provoke. See: Qūsī (n. 26), at 557.

her husband; do you understand?! Go declare this to your wives and brothers."[121]

A proof that those who seek unveiling indulge in quieting the voices of jealousy in their hearts, killing them in place of enjoying mixing with women other than their own, is that those among the believers who imitate them do not allow anyone to socialise with *their* women except those who allow them to socialise with their own women [in return]. If they had truly intended for the unveiling they call for to be an emancipation of women from the so-called "shackles" of veiling, then they would not uphold the condition of reciprocity in unveiling their women for any acquaintance.

Unveiling Has Now Become Half-Nakedness

Another obvious proof that the aim of modern unveiling among women is abnormal, incongruent with [positive] reform, signals that those who seek it do not do so in good faith, and which does not increase [women] in equality with men, is the fact that they [women] have [already] been created free, just as men have.

One proof of [the fact that this modern unveiling is abnormal, and does not make women more equal with men, similar to how they are already created free in nature like them,] is that their unveiling does not stop at men's limits. They uncover their arms to their armpits, chests, backs, and legs, while men consider it unnecessary to reveal [any of] these body parts at all.

Today's unveiling has gone beyond what the language originally intended–which is to reveal the face.[122] It has [instead] transformed to mean the half or one-third nudity we see now, and mixing with men in this state![123]

---

[121] Cenab Şehabeddin Bey attended a party held in honour of Delarue-Mardrus in France when he heard this from her verbally. Şehabeddin Bey was speaking over dinner with another French poet about women in the Muslim world, when Delarue-Mardrus interjected with her own opinion, recorded here. See: Şehabeddin Bey, Cenab. *Evrak-ı Eyyam*. Dar Sa'ādat–Qana'āt Matbaası, 1331/1915, 140-142.

[122] The term employed in Arabic for unveiling here is *sufūr*. This comes from the root *s-f-r*, which refers originally to revealing (*kashf*) but would also indicate sweeping (*kanasa*), scratching (*kashaṭa*), and to travel for which it is popularly employed (*safar*). Ibn Manẓūr mentions that the root, when it appears in the form *sufūr*, however, refers to "a woman who unveils (*safarat*) her face, meaning when the veil (*niqāb*) is lifted, revealing her face." See: Ibn Manẓūr, Muḥammad. *Lisān al-'Arab*. 3rd ed. Vol. 4. 10 vols. Beirut: Dār Ṣādir 4/367.

[123] Though there is a valid difference of opinion (*ikhtilāf*) among classical Muslim jurists with regards to a woman covering her face in public, the predominant (*mu'tamad*) position of the four Sunni schools of thought holds it to be an obligation. Jurists within the later Ḥanafī school, which is perhaps the most lenient in a woman's requirement for covering, held that safety from the fear of temptation (*khawf al-fitna*) should be guaranteed for a woman to reveal her face, and because this could not be guaranteed in the general public,

We can never permit this for a nation whose people care about their women's chastity. We see it as the vanguard of corruption and debauchery, and are shocked by writers who call for unveiling as a self-evident good. [Despite this,] time and time again we see them complaining about the breakdown, humiliation, and recklessness of women at summer resorts and beaches.

Poetic Descriptions of the Alexandrian Beaches

The impulsiveness of young men and women behind their gushing lust, especially at Stanley Bay [for example],[124] is described by one of the great poets of Egypt in a poem:

The eyes notice a herd of addax above the sand
Scattered upon it like a bouquet of roses

Swaying on their sides above its surface
Legs spread out, with curved flanks

You spot another [herd] gathered above the ocean
Like a flock of birds leaving their nests

And between themselves another, coming and going
Like the tides of the wave, high and low

Naked from all sides of the body, except
A part that too remains exposed, without [much] cover

A young girl sits in the club on [the lap] of a young boy

---

they argued that she should be required to cover it. The preeminent Ḥanafī legal authority Muḥammad Zāhid al-Kawtharī, Ṣabrī's adjunct as the last *Şeyhülislam* of the Ottoman Empire and who lived in exile alongside him in Cairo, states that "As for what has been narrated from leading [Ḥanafī] authorities (*fuqahā 'l-amṣār*) regarding the permissibility of a woman revealing her face and hands, [then] this is restricted to a lack of fear from temptation. Where is that civilised society in which a person may be guaranteed respite from temptation when a woman leaves [her home] unveiled?...And [while] the lack of temptation [may] be ascertained in a specific viewer, with regard to the majority of people, in front of whom the woman appears [with her face] unveiled, then the lack of fear from temptation cannot be envisioned for them altogether. [As such], prohibition from unveiling in front of them becomes necessary based upon this legal basis (*ta'līl*). It is through this that the [position of the] school of Abū Ḥanīfa (d. 150/767) and his companions becomes clear on the issue." See: al-Kawtharī, Muḥammad. *Maqālāt al-Kawtharī*. Cairo: al-Maktaba al-Tawfīqiyya, 230.

[124] Stanley Bay was a popular beach in Alexandria, Egypt during the 1930s.

Upon the rose; between the pouring, the glasses, and the wine

There the desires enveloping every pair
Everything humiliating in the open market

Genitalia in the sea, and likewise upon land
Woe to the loss of manners upon the land and sea

And another [poet] said:

Did you see the crows? Crowded
Above the coast, or swimming [in the sea]?

And you saw the beautiful women, walking in [their] splendour
Flaunting [their bodies] as they come and go

They were misguided seeing their mothers' [behaviour]
And [due to] the careless of [their] fathers

And their husbands, overlooking [their shamelessness]; out of weakness
Or through a corruption [i.e., cuckoldry] that lay within them

And [due to] their brothers, [themselves] drowning in desires
Careless of the path [taken] by their sisters

They [the women] lay off decency, thinking of it as
Tattered affairs and [worn-out] customs

And they expose their bodies, save a bit
Abandoning all shame in the way they move

Swaying as they come and go
Displaying their flirting without shame

They exceed in [playing around]; in fun and games
Not carrying around good customs or a [level] mind

At time you may notice them dancing
With [older] men, and with their own peers

And sometimes you see them on the sands
Stretched out besties a crowd of young men

Seducing [these] young men with their eyes
And with shaking flanks [i.e., hips] or the [seductive female] laugh

Sometimes they banter with one another without any shame
And at other times, they banter [similarly] with young boys

They hit one wave after another
Jumping lightly and squealing [displaying femininity]

A state [of affairs] that truly injures all virtue
And [at its sight], a righteous soul bleeds [in pain]

Stanley Bay, you are a [source of] shame for Egypt
And you are among its [ugliest] stains

Oh sea, cleanse the people and wash away
The evils you notice from them

And another [poet] said:

Here, we have now left; so tell me
What did you see at 'Stanley'?

What did you see as you stood
Early morning on the overlooking sand

From every laughing body
Invoking [of their] enjoyment to us

From every conqueror of the hearts
Striding in boastfulness, and coy

Or every dweller of the open
Or every resident of the shade

Crowds of great beauty
Going around; [playing] hard to get and [then] giving in

This one–greeting whomever she wishes
And that one–miserly rejecting others

The earth collapsed with me until
I almost disappeared from my place

Amidst my amazement, I started
Gawking at those receiving and turning

So when the alluring deer
Pass by, not affecting my likes

And when thin waists are greater
Than any statements and descriptions

And when sleeping eyelids
Can almost kill anyone

And when shining faces
Almost extinguish every mind

Oh heart, this is the Ka'ba–
Of the world, so stop and pray

For the naked harlots as if
They are mermaids of the great sea

From any valley in Kināna[125]
Or any [of its] places and stores

The unique beauty rose upon
The sands of the sunken beach

Whatever I say, I will not
Reach the bare minimum

Oh heart, as the beauty peaks
Let go of decency for today

And smile as does the desire
And break off every shackle

[125] Kināna, originally an Arab tribe situated near Makkah along the Tihāma coast, is often employed metaphorically in Arabic poetry referring to any 'place' in general.

Forget life and what is in it
And leave misery for that which distracts

Enjoy what is in front [of you]
Of women in a thousand forms

They wear the white waves
Of the ocean, except for some

And they swam so beautifully how
Disappearing in water and sand

And trading with passions
Going from one partner to another

They deceive, seducing thousands of men
With a single flirtatious smile

Such that hearts remain
Remembering [them] in travel and rest

This one wishes communion
While that wishes to forget

And the people from that which they were
Struck, by mistake and ignorance

Woe to the deer that
Chased away the dreams, woe to me!

In the intoxication of the beautiful dream
It became free of all sustenance

Who taught the petite deer
The ferocity of lions, tell me?!

The View of a Parliamentarian Writer

And about this, a writer from parliament mentioned that:

"This boy and this girl, by Allāh, are a young boy and girl from this civilisation, the effects from which we suffer. Both can be seen at the summer resorts coming out of their lodging cabins, at the break of dawn, naked. Their heads bare, their private parts brazenly exposed, they cross from the lodge to the beach in this fashion, then do not enter the water that it may cover their private parts, but rather wander the length of the beach or the sidewalk, as [one might imagine] the first humans might have done when they would leave their shelters to hunt for food. It is as if both of them [the primitive man and the beachgoer] are hunting prey, except that the nets they use are different.

[Unfortunately,] this assembly is made up of the sons of Adam and the daughters of Eve, by Allāh! It is an assembly of those sons of Adam deeply immersed into the heart of [modern] civilisation, and daughters of Eve infected with the opulence of the age, embellished from afar. You walk toward her to see what [more] remains latent, yet when you arrive near her, you see her nakedness, dancing the ugly dance of modern civilisation. If the soul cannot bear this torment [of modern degeneracy] in [closed] ballrooms and in splendid pageantry, then how can it bear to see it [stark] naked in the open like this?

Similar to this, one may see groups of people in twos, threes, or more than that, [who have their pictures taken] by a photographer in poses humiliating beyond all disgrace."

A Female Writer's Complaint Against the Consequences of Unveiling

And one female writer says:

"Fate and bad upbringing (*tarbiyya*) has given us some of these careless and mentally-deficient women who imitate the dancers by bathing at the beaches. Then, other women followed these women, such that the problem has become prevalent in all [social] classes, except those whom your Lord has protected. This careless woman walks on the beach as though possessed by a devil; she is openly, defiantly seductive. There is no law that can break her obstinacy, and nothing can curtail her defiance. She comes and goes in a tight, sleazy bathing suit, and sways, writhes, wobbles, and swaggers. She then looks at everyone sitting around her, and peruses their faces–what have all of these movements done to them, she wonders? Has looking at her delighted them or filled them with indignation?![126]

This woman is dumb, dull, and lifeless; she feels nothing, and she takes no heed of the beauties and joys of life. She is locked in chains and gives herself over to a mute, morose, and sombre existence. Her advocates say that too much pressure causes an explosion, and their prophecy has proven true.[127] So she runs about heedlessly and hurtles herself every which way, destroying the sanctuary of virtue and honour with the pickaxes of modern civilisation and ignorance. So from a loathed veil and a hidden stupor that no eyes see, [she goes] to the street unveiled, barefoot and naked. Modern civilisation whispers satanically and deceives her, so she imagines that a woman's freedom is freedom from modesty, and the crumbling of manners! The fathers and husbands were asleep and permissive, as were the authorities–none thought to terrorise, scare or prevent her [from falling into this misguidance].

Did it ever occur to anyone who calls for unveiling that women would go out to this extent? To sunbathe as they claim, naked of virtue and of clothes?

Had they taught them religion, their souls would have been purified of these lowly things. [If only they] had taught them religion, their steps would not have faltered; they would have a shield to safeguard them from the evils of corruption.

Did [those who call for unveiling] ever consider that the government and "noble" scholars would remain silent [when matters reached this extent]?!

---

[126] Modern readers might draw comparison with various other modern public facilities, such as mixed-gender gyms, which provides an indoor avenue for opposite genders to interact, and in certain cases, to seek attention. Cases of harassment in such establishments are relatively common too, with over 61% of women complaining to have been sexually harassed by men during their workout sessions. See: Hughes, Luke. "The Gym-Timidation Report: Exploring Gender Experiences in the Gym." Blog. OriGym, November 17, 2021. Last Accessed: December 15th, 2023. https://origympersonaltrainercourses.co.uk/blog/the-gym-timidation-report-exploring-gender-experiences-in-the-gym.

[127] Meaning, people forced to be uptight for too long will go to excess when restrictions are relaxed.

And did they ever think that the Agency of Publications[128] would need to oblige protective jealousy over decency and seek to prevent the publication of photos of women in bathing suits, leaving them as stacks of meat on the beaches?!

The careless woman takes joy in showing her body to the eyes of the public and their darting, treacherous glances. They bring one another to the beach, and grope [each other] without inhibition. This is not what our advocate Qāsim Amīn[129] sang about for us, this [trap] of woman's invention and to which she falls prey; had he known the unseen [i.e. the future] he would have cast her into the dark depths of a prison from which she could never escape. Qāsim wanted to teach women,[130] and sought for her to be equal with men."

We pause here for a moment, and say to the honourable writer:

In fact, this *is* what Qāsim Amīn and his ilk who call for unveiling were singing about. Anyone who has intellect and experience with men and women's desires, and their natural inclinations, knows that the result of unveiling will be these forms of disgrace. [Additionally,] we have come to this idea of unveiling through following the West, and we should have known that the unveiling of the Western woman did not remain confined to her face alone.

The fact that we have not yet learned from these shameful experiences caused by the callers to unveiling among us is reflected clearly in our assumption that the West's unveiling does not [necessarily] include

---

[128] This is in reference to one of the agencies (*idārāt*) working underneath the Armed Forces Logistics Authority (AFLA) of Egypt. This agency is responsible for administering censorship in the media and press derived from laws such as Article 10 of the Publications Law 20/1936 which states that, "'The cabinet has the right to ban publications offensive to religion or publications promoting erotica in a way that can disturb the public peace.'"

See: Ahram Online. "El-Sisi Moves on Banning Foreign Publications Offensive to Religion." News site. Ahram Online, January 14, 2015. Last Accessed: December 15th, 2023. https://english.ahram.org.eg/News/120255.aspx.

[129] Qāsim Amīn was an influential Egyptian aristocrat, jurist, writer, and leader of the Nahḍa movement. He was a determined advocate of women's rights, and a critic of veiling, gender segregation, early marriage and the lack of female education in the Arab world. He articulated his views famously in his book, *The Liberation of Women* (1899). Importantly, Amīn framed his feminist advocacy not as a rebellion against Islamic norms, but a return to true Islamic practice in conformity to a lost, Prophetic model of society. Ironically, despite his activism against veiling, Amīn was unable to persuade his own wife to stop wearing the face-veil (*niqab*). See: Baron (n. 44), at 37-38., Kholoussy (n. 39), at 50.

[130] Contrary to popular perception, Amīn did not advocate for gender-equal education; in his view, primary schooling was sufficient for women. The objective of education for women was also, in Amīn's view, not to qualify them for professional careers, but rather to make them better mothers and wives. Ṣabrī highlights the views of various liberal intellectuals during his time who proposed women's education for similar purposes, and proceeds to refute such notions. See: Kholoussy (n. 39), at 59f.

those humiliating negators of etiquette (*adab*) and good behaviour. It has become commonplace for reformers of unveiling and other issues to sit around, pontificating, and highlighting the difference between us and the Westerners in our propensity towards 'freedom.' They command us to take matters step-by-step until we can reach their level of knowledge and progress, however neither knowledge, nor progress, nor anything else will prevail over nature.

So unveiling to the extent of Western women–which has become the exemplar for the East today–and the mixing of women with men will certainly affect them, except in very rare cases, upon which no ruling is based.[131] And neither progression in unveiling, nor being poised for it, are anything but progression in corruption. If one is not 'poised' for something, one will not gravitate towards it. So these misleading statements from the advocates of unveiling, and the precautions they mention in order to justify their calls, should not deceive you.

Furthermore, I see that the noble writer is disappointed in women's lack of religious education, which would restrain and safeguard her from the evils of corruption, and yet despite that, [how strange that] she concurs with Qāsim Amīn's call towards the equality of women with men, something the religion of Islam does not accept [in the first place]?!

To this I say, in opposition to the writer: if they were to teach these women the religion according to their desired [interpretation], not shutting the doors of tribulations or [preventing] the means of corruption, such as unveiling and the mixing of the sexes–[a command] which is also part of the religion–then [that education] would not suffice as a guardian and an obstacle [from falling into these forms of debauchery].[132]

Some Fallacies of the Author of 'In Summary'

---

[131] Ṣabrī means that the rare cases of men, for instance, who are unaffected by mingling with women, are exceptions which prove the rule, and cannot be the basis for establishing general laws to govern society. As numerous jurists highlight, rules are derived from prevalent situations, not the rare. Ibn al-Qayyim (d. 751/1350) mentions in *Zād al-Ma'ād* that "rulings are [built around] dominant, prevalent [situations]; as for rare circumstances, they take the ruling of the nonexistent." The Ḥanafī jurist al-Sarakhsī (d. 483/1090), providing an example of the following principle, states in *al-Mabsūṭ* that "[like] the silence of a virgin, indicating acceptance, out of shyness built upon the predominant nature of virgins; as for the aberrant, then that is attached to the prevalent, dominant." See: al-Jawziyya, Ibn al-Qayyim. *Zād al-Ma'ād fī Hadyi Khayr al-'Ibād.* 27th ed. Vol. 5. 5 vols. Beirut–Kuwait: Mu'assasat al-Risāla–Maktaba al-Manār al-Islāmiyya, 1994, 5/374., al-Sarakhsī, Muḥammad b. Aḥmad. *al-Mabsūṭ* Vol. 2. 31 vols. Beirut, Lebanon: Maṭba'a al-Sa'āda–Dār al-Ma'rifa, 1989, 2/2.

[132] In fact, such reinterpretations would facilitate these corrupt activities with religious justification.

And the writer of *In Summary*[133] said:

> "In the lands which call towards 'freedom' there is an abundance of social instability. They are like a man sightless after a surgical procedure on his eyes; he cannot face the sun, and so needs brief flashes of light that increases bit by bit, until there comes a day where he can completely face the sun's splendour [i.e. they are slowly progressing towards total corruption]."

And this is the most eloquent explanation of what the advocates of progressive unveiling seek to accomplish. The meaning of this is that the antics at Stanley Bay, were they to be shown to the people of the nation twenty years later, for example, would not be seen as such a monstrosity then as they are seen today, even by the advocates of unveiling like this writer.

Look at his statement:

> "We used to praise Allāh[134] whenever we heard of a talented young Egyptian girl (he names here [in his article] some of whom studied in Europe).[135] We would praise and glorify Him. Those weak in vision and intellect say: this glorification and support of women is extreme.
>
> But in Stanley Bay lies their refutation;[136] for we must blow into the trumpet of virtues [i.e., pronounce them], and praise those women who sit for many years studying in their libraries,

---

[133] '*In Summary*' (*Mā Qalla wa Dalla*) was a series of articles written by the journalist Aḥmad al-Ṣāwī for the *Al-Ahrām* newspaper. These articles were later compiled and published as a book with the same title. al-Ṣāwī originally wrote for *al-Siyāsa* magazine, where one of his first articles 'The Emancipation of Women' caught the eye of Hudā Sha'rāwī. After summoning the young writer, and appraising him, she would fund his further studies in France where he would subsequently attain diplomas in journalism and the social sciences from Sorbonne Université, becoming one of the first to do so in Egypt. The editor-in-chief of *al-Ahrām* later, a Lebanese Christian named Anṭūn al-Gamayyil, would praise the open-minded liberalism found in al-Ṣāwī's writings, claiming that his studies in France were deeply influential in shaping his worldview. See: Yūsuf, Muḥammad Khayr Ramaḍān. *Takmilat Mu'jam al-Mu'allifīn*, Beirut, Lebanon: Dār Ibn Ḥazm, 1997, 1/149.

[134] By saying '*lā ilāha illa Allāh*'.

[135] Among the women mentioned by al-Ṣāwī are Suhayr al-Qalamāwī (d. 1997), a renowned literary figure and politician from Egypt. She was one of the first women to attend Cairo University and became one of the country's leading feminists. Al-Ṣāwī also mentions Na'īma al-Ayyūbī, daughter of the renowned Ottoman Palestinian historian Ilyās al-Ayyūbī, who like al-Qalamāwī was an early female student at Cairo University, and Egypt's first female lawyer. See: al-Ṣāwī, Aḥmad. *Mā Qalla wa Dalla.* Cairo, Egypt: Maṭba'a Dār al-Kutub al-Miṣriyya, 1934, 2/193.

[136] Ṣabrī is speaking here of "Stanley," the neighbourhood near downtown Alexandria and with which the beach is associated. His suggestion is that those women who are studying diligently in Stanley and such neighbourhoods refute those who criticise the virtues of women's rights, as opposed to those women walking upon its beaches.

expending their youth in service to society. It is they who prepare this society for a noble, sober, thoughtful freedom–not those who wear the slinky pyjama costumes of Stanley Bay."

What is strange is that Stanley Bay should be a refutation of those of weak intellect who oppose extremes in the glorification and support of women. Did the advocates of the modern woman not have a hand in the creation of Stanley Bay?! Why is it then that Stanley Bay is absent in the older generations in which the supporters of women and the callers to unveiling are not to be found?!

But through their virtue, and the virtue of supporting them, we have begun seeing next to those three distinguished women that the writer mentions, three thousand or more of those of whom he says:

> "so the Egyptian girl who believes herself to be the very epitome of elegance and grace, who has started sporting baggy beach pyjamas,[137] who exposes her thighs and breasts, her back and chest, who knows the secrets [of flirting], who has mastered modern dances, and she who knows how to play with words and hearts; this modern girl new to this modern freedom, does she know what she sings about?
>
> And the European woman, whom the Egyptian girl imitates today, is a woman from a country long-accustomed to freedom, a freedom which these countries bought with their blood, with women at the forefront. But does this [European] woman even know how to organise her house, or to sew her clothes? Or how to live by the *milleme* and the *dāniq* [i.e. to be thrifty]?[138] Or how to tighten her balance sheet? Or before any of this, how to raise her child? For she has bought her freedom at a heavy price, a price which has made her life a constant sacrifice and struggle; indeed, she bought her freedom at the cost of generations."

This talk concerning the abasement of the Eastern woman following [the West], and her excesses in unveiling and libertinism, has no

---

[137] al-Ṣāwī is likely referring to the distinctive style of women's swimwear popular in the 1930s. This style has become more common once again in recent years.

[138] The *milleme* was a small unit of currency which existed in Tunisia, Sudan and Egypt. The *dāniq* was a unit of currency equal to 1/6th of a dirham, which is used in a number of Arab countries today.

relation with the European woman knowing how to manage her house or to balance her budget, etc.

Perhaps the writer would forgive the Egyptian woman for her excessive humiliation and unveiling, if she knew what the European woman knows. What he should have said is: *the European woman is not as excessive in unveiling and being seduced by men.* However, he cannot say this, and were he able to, his statements outside of the subject would have sufficed him, such as, "[the fact that] the European woman is from a society long-accustomed to freedom, one that she has bought at a heavy price, does not justify the excessive unveiling of women."

Yes! Women of the East, especially Muslim women, have bought freedom at no price at all, by virtue of [sympathetic] volunteering male advocates.[139] And regardless of whether a woman gains her freedom cheaply, or at great expense, or none, and whether she be in the East or the West, her unveiling–in the modern sense of the word–is not without her own corruption.

I repeat my statement: one should not be deceived by the charming words of those who write on unveiling, capriciously contrasting our women and those of the Europeans. They suggest that unveiling does [European women] no harm, and falsely assume that our women, were they to 'progress' in kind, would also suffer no harm from unveiling–the sin, suggested therefore, is not in unveiling itself, but rather its poor implementation.

Digressions of this sort from the proponents of unveiling are merely intended to cover up the flagrant crime of unveiling with a veil of disinformation.

What is strange: is that it is [now] rare to find anyone, even among the pure-hearted, who is not deceived by this. So they believe in this [essential] difference between [European and Muslim] women, and they excuse through it the Muslim woman's unveiling to the degree it has reached today. They cling to hope for her progress like that of the European woman; that she breaks free from her present state of 'humiliation.' This thinking has become common, and no one has been spared its influence, even the

---

[139] Such individuals are sometimes referred to in modern vernacular English as 'simps', originally shortened from 'simpleton' whose first usage, with similar meaning, was found in 1903. The term appeared in the New York Times as early as 1923, in which a woman criticised timid, unmarried young men, saying that "those bachelor simps are afraid to take a chance..." Victor, Terry; Partridge, Eric; Dalzell, Tom (2006). *The New Partridge Dictionary of Slang and Unconventional English.* New York: Routledge. p. 1752. ISBN 0-415-25937-1., "Calls Bachelors 'Simps.': 'Afraid to Take a Chance,' Says Woman Referring to Club". *The New York Times.* 14 May 1923.

religiously grounded. I read a valuable article in a religious magazine where the writer masterfully explains Western civilisation's harms to the Egyptian woman.

In the course of this explanation, he states:

> "Aside from unrestricted liberalism, we have inherited from this civilisation another innovation (*bid'a*): cohabitation before marriage, which is now particularly widespread in Egyptian cities. We have begun emulating the Franks [i.e. the Europeans] in this type of preliminary [relationship] before marriage. Quite unfortunately, however, they are successful in their plans most of the time, whereas we are failures in practically all cases. They are advancing while we will *never* advance, even if we had all the time in the world. This is because they have ordered their plan precisely, and take their work very seriously; as for us, we approach this issue with no organisation, no system, nor any preparation, botching it in the worst ways possible."

What can be justly stated with regard to valuable articles [such as this] which exhort towards the proper path is: that cohabitation before marriage is harmful in every society, Eastern or Western. Establishing a 'system' will be of no benefit so long as a young man can [continue] isolating himself with a young woman.

And [this is] similar to what can justly be stated about modern unveiling: it harms both the Eastern *and* the Western woman. The [so-called] 'progress' of the Western woman does not protect her from its harms.

It is sufficient for both you and her: that she enters into these private soirées [appropriate to] her social status, and is embraced by [men] other than her husband, while dressed in an evening dress which does not cover but a small part of her body, and even reveals [by its tightness] what lies underneath the parts it *does* cover.

And it is enough for you to know about the 'progress' of Western civilisation that it considers protective jealousy–to which mankind is naturally disposed–a defect, pressing [people] to extricate themselves from it!

On the contrary, this thorough humiliation in exposing necks, chests, backs, shoulders, and thighs is nothing but a European construct. The

Eastern woman, particularly the Muslim woman, did not know this, and she learned it from the Western woman. Even the disgusting, abhorrent sight of Stanley Bay is itself a gift from the West.

Filth in Egypt or other [Muslim countries] was never previously as widespread in the land and sea; it was always contained in certain hidden corners. However, interspersed in between their rejection of the scandalous unveiling in the East, the West's Eastern proponents continue paying tribute to the Western woman. This is despite the fact that the Eastern woman took it [i.e., the scandalous unveiling] from her [Western counterpart] in the first place! They commend her [the Western woman] so that the fortified roots of [Western] imitation–that which the supporters of unveiling strove so hard to construct–is not destabilised.

One [should] be mindful of this. Do not listen to talk of the differences between the Eastern and Western woman, for [in doing so] you would become wholly accommodating of the effects of unveiling and the vile mixing of the two sexes.

And be warned: [against allowing] the deceivers to make you half their enemy, and half their supporter. My intention in writing on this topic is to bring attention to these salient points. Otherwise, how much has already been written against unveiling, even from its supporters when they are confronted with these disgraceful immoralities [sexual improprieties]? And most of these writers write more eloquently than myself.

On Premarital Acquaintance

We return to the statements of the writer of *In Summary*. He mentions [therein]:

> "What do we see in Stanley Bay? Is this Eastern temperance? Or is this Western temperance? It is neither this nor that! Rather it is a severely nefarious, bewildering, contradictory concoction, like the mixing of two arch-enemies, enemies both to one another, and enemies to themselves, like the devil.
>
> Woe to the culture which knows not its own creed! Its own school of thought! Its own fundamental principle! Its own religion! Here lies a conflict between temerity and hesitation, sexual impropriety and chastity, straightforwardness and roundaboutness, virginity and lewdness."

This writer [al-Ṣāwī], who is crying here about religion, responded elsewhere to a letter addressed to him in which someone wrote:

> "During my studies abroad, a strong friendship developed between me and a family there, which ended with me initiating an official engagement with a young lady from the family. However, I delayed the marriage pending my own family's approval, and I happened to return to Egypt during my break. I visited a friend of mine, and we began talking about marriage, and I gave him my news, and brought out a picture of my fiancée. He discouraged me from going ahead with it, and instead proposed to me the possibility of marrying a girl from his town; in fact we worked everything out [then and there], and I officially ended my engagement with the young foreign lady.
>
> My studies finished and I finally returned to my town. How great was my surprise when I found that one of my most honourable friends had usurped my [Egyptian] fiancée,[140] after he had told her family about me what Mālik said about alcohol![141]
>
> If young, marriageable women of middle-class stature were available in plentiful numbers, and in a way in which it was easy to get to know them, this marriage crisis (*azma li 'l-zawāj*) would not exist.[142] Nor would a friend transgress against his friend simply for coming across a young woman of moderate rank in knowledge, manners, beauty and wealth–that which we hope for in every wife.
>
> Can the respected columnist [al-Ṣāwī] assist us in demolishing this veil which separates one family from another, and work to refine some of our social customs?"

---

[140] Even proposing to someone already betrothed is prohibited in Islam by consensus. In a ḥadīth narrated by 'Uqba b. 'Āmir, the Prophet (ﷺ) states "A believer is the brother of another believer. It is not permissible for a believer then to make an offer while the transaction of his brother remains pending, or to make a proposal [to the same individual] with whom his brother's proposal is pending, until he [first] withdraws it." See: *Ṣaḥīḥ Muslim* (1414) Chapter: The Prohibition of Proposing Marriage when One's Brother has Already Proposed, Unless he Gives Permission or Gives up the Idea.

[141] This is a known expression in Arabic, more typically in the form "he said what Mālik had not even said about alcohol!" Referring to the 2nd/8th century Medinese jurist *Imām* Mālik b. Anas' extremely severe stance against any activity related to alcohol. The implication in this case is that the man's friend had been telling the girl's family terrible things about him.

[142] For more on the marriage crisis of late-19th and early-20th century Egypt, see: Kholoussy (n. 39).

– 'A. J.

So the writer responded to him as follows:

> "This is an old, chronic disease which we have dealt with often, and its pains always return. We have spoken about this matter so much we have grown bored. However, this dangerous crisis which young men and women are passing through in Egypt is the only thing capable of resolving this disgraceful situation quickly, definitively, wisely, and to the advantage of the Egyptian family.[143] We won't be satisfied with thousands of young, intelligent, pure Egyptian women perishing in the corners of [their] homes, their youth shrivelling away, spending their lives in apprehension, fantasies, and false hopes, ending up hopelessly trapped in meaningless and ignorant marriages. It is as though they have committed crimes for which they must now expiate!
>
> The idea that free-mixing leads to chaos is a trite, baseless position. Corruption in its *present* form is very foul. Young men have become satisfied with bachelorhood because it costs them little, whereas it costs young women their youth, which is the most precious thing they own."
>
> – al-Ṣāwī

Look at how he rates opposition to free-mixing as loathsome, all while it is in accordance with the position of Islam! Make him see the shameful behaviour of the people of Stanley Bay. They know not any creed, or ideology, nor principle, or religion.

Does the writer [himself] have an ideology on which he stands?[144]

Which religion permits free-mixing and cohabitation before marriage? We have already narrated some distasteful complaints about cohabitation from the other writer, who was sincere in his faith.

---

[143] al-Ṣāwī means that yes, there is some difficulty created by the modern changes in Egyptian life, but it is the only solution for the problems caused by the traditional system, which he holds to be worse.

[144] Ṣabrī asks rhetorically whether the author has any basis for his opinion in Islamic law, within the purview of the four main legal schools. In Islamic legal theory, all actions can be qualified according to a legal ruling ranging from obligation to prohibition, on the basis of explicit religious textual sources or analogical comparison with said sources.

We also heard criticisms of cohabitation directly from the mouths of some Christians while we were in Greece,[145] and the writer who says that the present turmoil is loathsome does not understand that the situation will become much worse when free-mixing is expanded, as he would so love. Perhaps storms of young men and women would go to Stanley Bay to spend their days of cohabitation before marriage, and do there what might otherwise happen in marriage.

It is strange that the writer, after seeing and criticising Stanley Bay, says that there is no proof that free-mixing leads to chaos, when Stanley Bay is nothing but an exhibition of free-mixing [and chaos].

Does the heedless questioner–who complains about the veil and seeks free-mixing, all while complaining about his friend who usurped his betrothed–not realise that free-mixing paves the path to [the scenario of] a friend usurping his friend's ***wife***, not just his fiancée?

As for how the writer says, "We won't be satisfied with thousands of young, intelligent, pure Egyptian women perishing in the corners of [their] homes, their youth shrivelling away," this is a preposterous misrepresentation slung [by him and his like] which conflates the present marriage crisis to what it would naturally entail of premarital cohabitation. He calls Egyptians to put their women up for sale and shove them onto the streets to find husbands, and for them to fling themselves into the arms of [random] men, to love and cohabit with them for a time before marriage.

This is despite the fact that the author and his likes know [very well], as well as they know their own children,[146] that the marriage crisis is worse in nations that permit their daughters to cohabit before marriage with whichever young men they like. This is because the young men who taste the sweetness of this cohabitation and become attached to it are in no need of marriage, and they have before them such various means by which to choose a partner [for cohabitation]. Or perhaps, this life of free-mixing with young women has shaken their trust in them, and made them wary of marriage. Instead, they settle for something that resembles it, and young women allow this by providing them their love.

---

[145] Muṣṭafā Ṣabrī spent a number of years in Greece following the establishment of the Turkish Republic after the First World War. He lived there in exile, later moving on to Romania, and finally to Egypt where he settled for the rest of his life. While living in the Greek city of Patras, he was reportedly received with great respect and admiration by many Orthodox Christian clergy. It seems likely to the translators that the Christians from whom Ṣabrī heard criticism of cohabitation were the clergy of Patras. See: Gharad (n. 11), at 140.

[146] This phrase is borrowed from the Qur'ān, "Those We have given the Scripture recognize this Prophet as they recognize their own children. Yet a group of them hides the truth knowingly." [*al-Baqara*: 146]

And yes, the young women also enjoy [the young men's] temporary love that lasts as long as their cohabitation; their youth hardly 'shrivels up in the corners of their home,' fruitlessly.[147]

So would this replacement [for marriage] which they attain please the writer who champions their interests?

As for their position after the market of this life [of temporary cohabitation] closes [and they drift] into stagnation, whether by returning to the corners of their homes–only now resembling widows, or by remaining 'available' upon the streets...well, does that not concern our social columnist?

Premarital Cohabitation Makes Marriage Difficult

The truth is that premarital cohabitation makes marriage difficult,[148] and makes it compete with something else like it, which is the opposite of what those supporters of unveiling and free-mixing claim.

So much so, that these cohabitating women who resemble wives mix with women veiled in their homes, and consequently prevent their marriage as well, just as they corrupt marriage for themselves.[149] The mistake and preposterous misrepresentation of the columnist are built on this [fact].

If all of them were to return to their houses and veils, young men would find no young women to manipulate; they would be forced to restrain [themselves]. The marriage market would thrive as it once did before the habit of premarital cohabitation was transferred from the West to some of our Muslim daughters.

And why doesn't the petitioner [who wrote to al-Ṣāwī] choose to marry one of these unveiled women already suitable for cohabitation [through prior experience] who are so plentiful in Egypt? [They are found] in such numbers that the author of the [earlier] article in the religious magazine complained about this innovation proliferating in her own lands,

---

[147] What Ṣabrī means is that young women are not the hapless victims of men, but willing partners in crime, who seek out sex and companionship. A woman's youth is unlikely to pass her by without her seeking these out through licit, or illicit means.

[148] The Institute for Family Studies reports that premarital cohabitation directly correlates to increased divorce trends in marriages for women. This also increases with the amount of sexual partners a woman has had before marriage; women having 0-1 partners were the least likely to divorce, with more directly relating to increased chances for divorce. See: Wolfinger, Nicholas H. "*Counterintuitive Trends in the Link Between Premarital Sex and Marital Stability.*" Blog. Institute for Family Studies (blog), June 6, 2016. Last Accessed: December 15th, 2023. https://ifstudies.org/blog/counterintuitive-trends-in-the-link-between-premarital-sex-and-marital-stability

[149] What Ṣabrī means is that 'loose' or divorced women have often had bad experiences with men, and so negatively influence younger women to not get married at all, or seek divorce.

so why can't the petitioner suffice with them? He seeks to bind together righteous women with corrupt ones, so that he can choose his wife from among the uncovered, yet find one still close to veiling [and what it represents]![150]

Listen to another petition raised by a doctor to the author of *In Summary*:

> "What I read today and yesterday about the incident of two doctors pained me. However, do you not believe that evil is present in every place? And were it not for evil, we would not feel any goodness either.
>
> Have you forgotten that these types of evil souls are found in every profession and craft? And yes, we are obligated to stand up to one who belittles the honour of a family with which he is entrusted–but what is your opinion, dear friend (*'azīzī*), on my painful situation which I described to you three years ago?
>
> I spent over twenty years in love with a girl whom I had not spoken with even once in my life. I secured an official engagement from her father, but he died, and with him all his promises. I [then] sought her from her brother, but he delayed [any progress for] five years. Because of this girl whom I knew nothing about, except that I had seen her before, and was pleased with her family's status, manners and character, and for her sake alone, I passed over great opportunities –both in Egypt and Europe–for over twenty years, because I [used to] believe that one day she will realise that I want her as a wife. So I stood fast by my word to her for twenty years or more.
>
> At last, I finally agreed with her brother last summer in Alexandria, her city, that I would not ask him anything about her inheritance from her father, and that I will, from my side, provide all the required furniture for the house.[151] This was so that I would not force him to bear even a single expense in order to prepare his sister [to be wed]. In fact, I purchased everything, down to the

[150] What Ṣabrī means is, why do these men put the good women with the bad? In his estimation, it is so that they can choose a wife from a wide spread of unveiled women, and socialise with them, but find one still modest at heart and close to the modest spirit of *ḥijāb*.

[151] It is customary among Egyptian Muslims and Christians, today and in Ṣabrī's time, for a prospective groom to own a house/apartment while the bride's family would fully furnish it before their wedding. In this case, the man in the story took on even the bride's family's responsibilities to make the marriage process easier.

packets of salt and pepper, and in doing so spent more than 280 [Egyptian] pounds.[152] I wrote to him about this so he could come and see for himself what I had purchased, and so that he could choose for his sister any apartment in any neighbourhood of Cairo. Do you know what he did? He didn't even respond!

Finally, my sister wrote to his mother, and the response, after twenty years, was: it is not possible for her to be married before her older sisters, and there are four of them!

And what is more ridiculous, she told my sister that, 'a fortune telling woman has told us that the marriage would be terrible. The best thing I can tell your brother is to search for another spouse. As for the stuff he bought, he can do with it as he pleases!'

So I waited twenty years to hear the verdict of a fortune teller! And I bought everything because I took a promise from someone I thought to be honourable.

You may say: why didn't you contact her directly? To which I would respond: this is something impossible, because these women are living in the 18th century, in a house that looks like a fort from the Middle Ages! She doesn't even know what a cinema is, and finds it strange that [some] women go out [of their homes] unveiled! She's from Alexandria, lives there too,[153] and has yet to even see the beach!

I used to dream that I would show her the world, and expose her to it while she was still raw. But I erred, dear friend, because I forgot that our two souls might perhaps not be destined (by the 'stars') to entwine. In reality I did not know her, and yet imagined her for twenty years to be an angelic wife; I imagined her as "An Ideal Wife,"[154] and just like that wasted my life. The fortune teller destroyed my hopes. A fortune teller decided the future of a young man living in Europe, from an educated family which couldn't be further from this hocus-pocus!

---

[152] According to our calculations and use of historical inflation calculation tools, this would amount to about $20,350 in 2023, which is equal to E£628,833 as of this writing.

[153] Alexandria in the early 20th century was likely the most cosmopolitan, liberal and Western-influenced city in Egypt. The letter-writer is likely emphasising her seclusion by pointing out that she is living in Alexandria of all places, as opposed to a rural village one might expect for such a person.

[154] The author of the letter himself mentioned "An Ideal Wife" in English. It is suggestive that in his letter, written entirely in Arabic, his conception of an ideal wife is something he found easiest to express in English, rather than his native language.

So what do you think? I am a doctor;[155] don't you see that in our society there are still many people who care about honour, honesty, and fidelity?

-Dr. Maḥmūd

So he [al-Ṣāwī] responded:

I do not doubt for a single moment, dear brother, that doctors are fine examples of noble character. Rather, their class is one of the most noble and generous in our society.

As for your issue, it is as dangerous as it is sad. For you saw a young girl, sacralized her, and made her your hope and desire. Then you travelled, grew up, studied, all in hopes of marrying her. [But] she did right by you, treating you with beauty–without you [even] knowing; [this is because] she protected you from so much evil. She took you by the arm [i.e., she was the reason] and made you focus on the sciences [your studies], she made you succeed, and made you into a useful, working man for your country. You saw the whole world without forgetting her; what would you call that? It certainly is fidelity, however, in another place [than where it was sought]. You now seek fulfilment from someone who either had no will or no thought in the matter, or someone who forgot you entirely. She herself does not claim all this loyalty [from you] after a mere innocent, youthful glance. So why does your blood boil, and why do you trap yourself in a tight prison with a phantom that doesn't exist?! I'm certain that if you were to see her today, you would reject her, because there is a vast gap between your upbringing and hers; you have travelled and seen the world while she doesn't even know anything about Alexandria. The opportunities in front of you are auspicious, for there are many girls of your country who would love for you to open the doors of happiness for them. So take advantage of what

[155] The petitioner is intimating that if something so ridiculous could happen to him, while he practises medicine–one of the highest, most respected professions in society–then what does that say about anyone less, and of a society in general that heeds the wishes of a fortune-teller over a respectable professional?

remains of your life, and Allāh will send someone else to rescue that martyred girl.[156]

-al-Ṣāwī

It was incumbent upon the gentleman (*ustādh*),[157] the columnist, to consider or think on the state of this petitioner, whom he admits is an example of noble character, and who does not seek his help in tearing down the *ḥijāb*. It was incumbent upon him to think and consider: What was it that compelled a young man studying in Egypt and Europe–full of tempting, uncovered women–to remain tied twenty years to this young girl in Egypt with whom he had not met except once or twice, or spoken a single word, and about whom he knew nothing except the respectable station of her family? A woman who has never heard of the cinema, and is bewildered at how respectable women now go out uncovered–all while being from Alexandria, living there, and having yet to [even] see the beach! Is this not the magic of the *ḥijāb*? Of course! It is this *ḥijāb* which made her seem like an angelic wife to him; the uncovered beauties did not fill his eyes; [instead, the *ḥijāb*] made him consider them to be disgraceful [by comparison].

I have recounted at length, as is my habit, from a number of writers, especially the writer of *In Summary*. I have done so so that those who read my article[s] do not hear my words alone. Rather, they also hear those in the opposition who have not yet been critiqued, particularly those whose words people care [dearly] about, along with a few words from supporters or neutral parties whose words support my claims–all of that in a single article.

The Accountability of the Permissive Husband

The writer of *In Summary* also says (and this is the last of what I will quote from him):

"I once saw a virtuous man, possessed of excellent focus and sound manners, dragging his small son with his hand, both moving sluggishly, as though each were a burden upon the other. The father entered the grocery store around lunchtime to get prepared food in a sealed container, or perhaps cheese, olives, and sweets, because his house was without a woman!

---

[156] The girl was "martyred" in the sense that, because of her family, she lost the opportunity to marry someone as well-established and distinguished as the doctor, while remaining unmarried herself.

[157] The title *ustādh* technically means 'professor' but is used colloquially in Egypt for any respectable adult man, effectively meaning something equivalent to 'gentleman' or 'sir.'

Why? Did the mother of this child pass away? Of course not! However, she was worse than a dying woman. As it happens, she's a foreign woman whom this man sheltered and gave his name [i.e., married her] after the people of her town had driven her out. He would deprive himself [so they could afford] for her to travel to Europe every summer to visit her family. But this did not prove to be anything positive for her; rather she left their children with him, seeking divorce. They did, in fact, divorce, and she [subsequently] married his friend.

If she were Egyptian, there would have been some doubt in the matter. We used to say [in such situations]: her family must have married her off to a scoundrel who doesn't deserve love. But she was a foreigner; she migrated from her homeland purely out of her own choice, and knew her [ex-]husband for months or years before she married him.

This harlot exchanges men as she pleases. She took a man's youth and gave him children, then she restrained herself from him, withdrawing and forsaking him and the children to take another man's youth, and to give him children as well.

The sin is not hers alone of course, indeed it is also the sin of he who seduced her, for how can a man who enters his friend's house and has no problem seeing his [friend's] wife with traitorous eyes, then have a problem causing her to divorce? [Such a man] does not care about his friendship, and he makes a mockery of the sanctity of marriage, of motherhood and fatherhood. How should such a man be judged?!

Truly dignified masculinity (*al-murū'a*) necessitates that if he sees even a seedling of this deplorable love, he should flee, placing a barrier between himself and [that love], for within [it] is destruction and desolation.

What is more painful for the soul than to see a man dragging his and his child's feet on the streets to buy food from the grocer, food that is tasteless for him, because he has been stabbed in his heart by a dagger at the hand of his friend, and that of his [now ex-]wife?!

– al-Ṣāwī

The writer forgets when he writes, "The sin is not hers alone of course, indeed it is also the sin of he who seduced her, for a man who enters his friend's house and has no problem seeing his [friend's] wife with traitorous eyes,..." that there is a third sinful person: the man whom the writer laments over, i.e., the man who allowed his friends to socialise with his wife. She may have possessed angelic beauty, but could never possess an angelic disposition,[158] and likewise the friends. While forgetting the third sinner, he [also] neglects to mention the very basis of the sin and corruption, and that is unveiling and free-mixing. With that, the writer has forgotten the fourth sinner as well, which is *everyone* who calls to and defends unveiling by speech or pen.

God does not forgive this [fourth] sinner, even if he forgives the earlier ones! The peak of all puzzlement is that the writer does not see the glances of the friends who socialise with the man's wife to even be treacherous by nature, in the sense that it [this glance becoming treacherous] is simply the natural outcome of a [carnal] disposition triumphant over everything else!

So this story, published by the pen of an author who is among the chief enemies of the *ḥijāb*, is a sharp, definitive proof (*ḥujja*) against them. No matter how much they may deny the clear truth, persisting upon their call, [the truth] will undoubtedly disgrace them by the witnessing tongue,[159] as seen, for example, at Stanley Bay! They cannot avoid destroying their homes by their own hands, as witnessed by the author of *In Summary* in this recounting.

On How Westerners are Accustomed to Seeing Exposed Women

---

[158] In mainstream Islamic theology, angels are considered sinless and are not known to be capable of disobeying Allāh whatsoever. See: al-Qurṭubī, Muḥammad. *al-Jāmiʿ li Aḥkām al-Qurʾān*. Vol. 2 20 Vols. Cairo, Egypt: Dār al-Kutub al-Miṣriyya, 1964, 2/52.

[159] What Ṣabrī means is that these spectacles of unveiling and free-mixing, such as what is witnessed at Stanley Bay, stands as a proof against those that call toward unveiling. They may believe that unveiling can be positively liberating for women, a means for them to use the opportunity to cultivate and educate themselves, and it may be argued that these perverse environments are aberrations from the norm, or that they can be explained away as existing for some other reason. The truth, as Ṣabrī indicates, is that these spectacles are the direct effect of unveiling, and simply their natural result. He condemns unveiling, citing Stanley Bay, for example, as a self-evident proof ("witnessing tongue") against those who believe unveiling would lead to anything else, or those that attempt to provide farfetched explanations for their existence.

Another lie of those who [attempt to] minimise the harms of unveiling for the Eastern woman who imitates the Western woman, is their statement that:

> "The Western man, since he sees women with many bare limbs from [his] childhood and is raised among them, is not agitated by the sight of those limbs, whereas it agitates the Eastern man unfamiliar with their sight, who is new to this lifestyle."

This is an outright lie, even if it resembles the truth insofar as it includes warning the Eastern woman from imitating the Western one. In fact, you might even be led to believe it was said by the enemies of unveiling. However, from another perspective, [this point of view] will be permissive for her [the Eastern woman] in the future if the unveiled lifestyle progresses amongst us, and our men's eyes become familiar with [women's bare skin]. Rather, the core of [this point of view] seeks [to create a culture of] permissiveness around unveiling in the current day by lightening its [burdensome] presence in the souls [of Easterners], and pacifying them with [the promise of] future familiarity. Despite this, it is built upon a false claim: that men in the West are not concerned [or aroused] by the sight of women unveiling their attractive limbs there.

So do the women of the West, when they beautify and flaunt [themselves] as they do, only do so in vain? Have they no goal when doing so? Do they not have desires [they seek] within men?

And is there also no desire for women on the part of the men who laid the foundations of Western civilisation and created its social protocols? [That which] includes dance parties with the women, [where they can] hold their waists clad in the most revealing, beautiful dresses?

Have they, the men, simply lost their minds?

Or have they, the women, simply lost theirs?

Or [is it the case that] those among us who claim that "the 'clothed naked woman'[160] in the West does not arouse man's desire, or even catch his eye," are simply messing with the minds of Muslim Easterners?!

---

[160] This is referencing a ḥadīth narrated by Abū Hurayra in which the Prophet (ﷺ) says that in an age after his own, there will be "women who are clothed, yet appear to be naked," who will be condemned to the hellfire. See: *Ṣaḥīḥ Muslim* (2128) Chapter: Women Who Are Clothed Yet Naked, Turning Away From Righteousness And Leading Others Astray.

The truth: is that this strange, perplexing intrepidity among the callers to unveiling merely reveals to you the [advanced] stations they have achieved in their bold excursions into heedless chattering.

Stranger still: is the adoption of their position by many intelligent people, despite its being so feeble that it does not stand up to even the slightest investigation or [critical] thinking.

Yes! Certainly, the West is well-familiar with the excesses of women as regards unveiling and free-mixing with men, and also of the corruption it entails. [It is only] the heedless person who may be led to believe that unveiling and free-mixing do not produce in those lands what they are bound to do by their very nature.

In glancing at what has preceded,[161] we have made abundantly clear that women who uncover do not suffice with unveiling their limbs at the same limits as men, all while they pursue their 'equal rights' with men. There must be some significance, then, in this great difference between the two in clothing and nakedness [when given the choice, despite the call to equality in everything]. And it must be the case that the significance of [women's] inclination toward nakedness, East and West alike, is to be consumed by the viewers' gaze. And even if we were to overlook this intention [being consciously present] within them, this 'consumption' would be attained regardless.[162]

And so the divine Islamic law, which states that "the eyes fornicate, and the limbs fornicate,"[163] along with the disposition of a Muslim man who jealously guards his honour, will never accept the enjoyment of [his] woman in any way by anyone who has no right to do so.

Critique of Claims Regarding Dancing & Its Benefits

---

[161] Referring to the section on how unveiling has become half nakedness.

[162] What Ṣabrī means is, even if one does not acknowledge that this is what women want, they still get the satisfaction of being seen.

[163] This narration can be found with various wordings. Among them is the narration of Ibn 'Abbās where the Prophet (ﷺ) states that, "Allah has written for the son of Adam his inevitable share of adultery whether he is aware of it or not: The adultery of the eye is the looking (at something which is sinful to look at), and the adultery of the tongue is to utter (what it is unlawful to utter), and the innerself wishes and longs for (adultery) and the private parts turn that into reality or refrain from submitting to the temptation." See: *Ṣaḥīḥ al-Bukhārī* (6612) Chapter: 'It is impossible for a society which We have destroyed to ever rise again,...' 'None of your people will believe, except those who have believed, already...' 'And they will beget none but wicked disbelievers.'

And among the clear follies (*'abath*) of the mind was something I read in the newspapers citing an article from the Western magazine *Reader's Digest*, which enumerates the traits with which a modern man must be endowed:

> "...Likewise, the young man should learn dancing, for it is in one respect bodily exercise, and in another an art which cultivates a virtuous soul, and familiarises one's sight to the fairer sex through eyes devoid of vileness and lust..."

It is understood from this: that Western civilisation cowered before those who stood firm for [the idea that] vice should be sold as virtue in its marketplace.

The reason for the marketability of this sale is that it includes material pleasure for the transactors, violating modesty in its path, and calls for habituation to one's sexual desires as a virtue, independent from lust and vileness! It is excessively bold, and denigrates the virtue of Islam which prevents women from mixing with strange men, such that in this regard Islam would need to be defended from the infringements of these frivolous people, all while [defending] this Western civilisation, which destroys [true] virtue, and is founded upon the principle of fulfilling one's sexual needs, from being blameworthy and deficient itself!

This flipping of realities makes fashionable the Westerners' strict adherence to their well-known culture, while misguiding Muslim children from their straight path.

And even if there were no support from the strength of any Western power behind this free-mixing lifestyle, it would still count as a black mark upon any nation that chooses it.

It is for this reason that the issue of women is the greatest barrier between Islam and Western civilisation, so the Muslim man will not accept a naked, mixed [public] life with Muslim women, so long as his Islam is sound. [Meanwhile,] the Westerner does not see any greater inhibition to him adopting Islam than the *ḥijāb* of women,[164] even if he may not doubt in

---

[164] Even today, the *ḥijāb* remains one of the key issues of cultural controversy surrounding the Muslim diaspora in Western countries. The European Network Against Racism reports disproportionate discrimination against Muslim women in all areas of society in Europe. In France, for example, 79% of the population reported that the headscarf was a problem for 'vivre-ensemble' (living together), while nearly 65% of Swedes reported feeling that Muslim women were oppressed. An overwhelming majority of recorded Islamophobic crimes in Europe also take place against Muslim women, with most wearing over religious

[Islam's] being the religion most deserving to be accepted. [This is] because it is difficult for him to turn away from the life mixed with women to which he has grown accustomed, and which is highly advantageous to his lower self. This is not [even] to mention that the non-Muslim Westerner, even your wannabe-European (*mutafarnij*)[165] will not show you sincere love and kindness once he sees that you will not allow him to mix freely with the women of your home and sit with them, whether in your presence or absence.

We return to the columnist's statement, "so the men who attend dance parties flush with lights, and who embrace half-naked women, are so few as to be nonexistent."

Based on the premise of the columnist, we might infer that it is as though they were embracing pieces of wood, not aroused in the slightest by those erotic women. Perhaps it is easier for those who believe rubbish like this to put a veil on their [own] minds than on women, may they be damned.[166]

And that magazine column reminded me of what I once read in some Turkish newspapers a few years ago–the newspapers at that time would compete in scrambling to appease their godless government[167]–which sought women's unveiling and free-mixing with men:

> "Certainly no one in this free-mixed, open lifestyle glares at anyone else's wife [with bad thoughts], and those [supposed] evils one can envision within [that life] only spring [into the minds] of those who have not been educated in the social customs [of high-society], and whose sensitivities have neither developed nor progressed.
>
> Yes! Certainly, a man at his first entry to that life, when he sees beautiful naked women near him, is flabbergasted and ashamed, then overcome by his lower self that incites to evil (*al-*

---

symbols, such as the *ḥijāb*. Hatred and fear of the headscarf has grown so much, affecting all aspects of secular life and society, that many sociologists even term this phenomenon 'hijabophobia.' See: European Network Against Racism. "Forgotten Women: The Impact of Islamophobia on Muslim Women." ENAR, 2016. Last Accessed: December 15th, 2023.
https://www.enar-eu.org/wp-content/uploads/factsheet9-european_lr_1_.pdf.

[165] The word *mutafarnij* literally means someone who seeks to be an *ifrinjī*, or Frank, to use the archaic Arabic term for European.

[166] Ṣabrī is saying here that these people think it is easier to put a veil of modesty upon the minds of men, such that they will not have sexual thoughts when touching attractive women, than to put a physical veil on the bodies of women.

[167] In 1928 the government of Turkey removed a provision from the 1924 provision which recognized Islam as the religion of the state in its constitution; thereby beginning Turkey's history as an officially secular nation.

> *ammāratun bi 'l-sū'*). However, the one who has become accustomed to this life, mature in feeling and sensitivity, can, for example, enter thermal hot springs by the sea and look upon the beach, or the shore where the water does not exceed a handspan, and behold the most exquisite naked women–but neither the lure of the devil, nor the soul's incitement would even enter his mind.
>
> And this [same] man can dance at soirées with women who appear almost naked, his eyes piercing hers, and his body intertwined with hers, without feeling anything stir in him; on the contrary, he can train his otherwise weak impulsivity in the presence of the woman, ripening and nurturing his commanding soul [in order to balance between maintaining respect for women, while also developing sexual attraction towards them, to be exhibited in appropriate circumstances]. As such, in this civilised life, there is both the protection of [one's] chastity as well as self-satisfaction.
>
> One such man well-established in this life told me that one day he saw his wife [chatting] with a cook from his house named Tusun, while she was uncovered, and he prohibited her [from doing so again]. From what I knew of him, he would bring his wife every night to [social gatherings with] his friends who would [subsequently] dance and speak with her in private, so naturally I was surprised by what he said. I asked him, "aren't you the one who brings her to everyone uncovered?" He responded that "they can't be compared with the cook Tusun because they know to respect the woman, while he considers her as something to be consumed–like a pear."

Look what this writer says and learn, if you do not already know, that "those who mix and dance with women clasped in their arms, intend thereby to train their unruly souls, and to accustom them to restraining their sexual desires," then combine this statement with [what was mentioned by] the Western columnist,[168] and be astounded by them both!

---

[168] Ṣabrī intends to show the contradiction between the two contentions. If these dance parties are meant to tame people's desires, while simultaneously meant to cultivate them, what is their true purpose?

Those Accustomed to Mixed Gatherings Vs. Those New to the Custom

It may occur to you that the one accustomed to sitting with women in close proximity will not be like someone new to this arrangement and [social] context, and that becoming accustomed to and repeating something is not like starting it. These two writers have depended on deceiving the reader into [believing] in the existence of a difference between these two states, and we will not simply pass over this point, as it happens to be one of the most unique points [brought up] in support of unveiling, and because those who call towards unveiling rely on [this point] to buttress their falsehoods. And in spite of being extremely false, this [point] most resembles the truth, so we will not pass over it without giving it its due consideration. It is in [response to] such that our statement on the issue of unveiling can be distinguished. And so we state that:

It is necessary for vigilant Muslims to question these sophistic proponents [of unveiling], who wish to drag people down to the depths of idiocy: 'if those who brought about the modern mixed lifestyle did so in order to erase the effect of one sex upon the other, and to crush their mutual sexual attraction, then what is the purpose behind this situation that rests in contradiction to natural [human disposition and] order? What benefit is reaped from it? Especially [when one considers that] public interest and welfare (*maṣlaḥa*) lies in bringing about pleasures for them, not in destroying them! What is the benefit in lowering the worth of one sex in front of the other by removing the fervour of attraction between them and replacing it with coldness and stagnancy?

We then state:

Yes, someone accustomed to something is not like someone new to it, except that there is an extremely important point that must be noted: The relationship of a man and a woman gathered for reasons pertaining to attraction, whether it is limited to simply sitting with her, or drawing close in her arms while twirling and dancing; no matter how many times this is repeated, will not calm his sexual inclinations, nor put them to rest. Rather the opposite it will be the case, it would increase them, making them more extreme.

No matter the degree to which your relationship with women increases, no matter how much you increase the numbers and types [of such relationships], you would still not be satisfied. Rather you would have added thirst upon thirst, so the intended effect of becoming [platonically] accustomed would end up becoming the opposite. If there is anything in the world that, no matter the amount of it that is achieved, it would never make one content, nor it would ever suffice from reaching its purpose, then that would be meeting a woman and [having] her touch.

And how true is what the poet says:[169]

And when you sent your glance surveying
A day for your heart, did the sights tire you?

Did you see that which you could not
Achieve in full, nor be patient for even some of it?[170]

So based upon that, the claim of security from *shayṭān's* lure and the incitement of the commanding soul when a man meets a woman, and that its effects are dissipated by repeated meeting and the soul's becoming accustomed to the new, civilised life of cohabitation is **false**, and should not be heeded.

Yes, perhaps the [the idea that] the eyes could achieve some type of satiety, and that feelings of sexual affinity could be deafened at the sight of many women and by playing with them *can* be accepted, but [only] under one condition: that their natural results [i.e. sex] should adjoin these preliminaries, such that the [sexual] ardour of modern men could [also] be sufficed there, and that their obstinate desires would find rest.[171] However, securing chastity this way within this new lifestyle is like replacing a guarantee [i.e., veiling that would definitely protect women] with a total lack

---

[169] These lines of poetry were composed by a young woman that the poet al-Asmaʿī noticed while circumambulating (performing *ṭawāf*) around the Kaʿba. He kept staring at her as if she were an addax (a white antelope) in the desert. As his eyes remained captured by her beauty, she said these verses. See: Sibṭ b. al-Jawzī, Shams al-Dīn Yūsuf. *Mir'āt al-Zamān fī Tawārīkh al-Aʿyān*. 1st ed. Vol. 14. 23 vols. Damascus, Syria: Dār al-Risāla al-'Ālamiyya, 2013, 14/90.

[170] [Muṣṭafā Ṣabrī]: And even if it was the case that the age of unveiling and free-mixing has not destroyed the passionate love (*al-ʿishq*) of past ages, that which would lead to the madness of the passionate lover, or even to his death, we would still say: certainly this [type of] relationship with a beautiful, upright woman, when a man is with her in these soirée halls, places him squarely within the talons of passionate love, killing him or reducing him to madness. However, the age of unveiling and free-mixing is one of the woman's debasement. It suffices both sexes of the need for passionate love [in the first place], and it confirms the statement of the poet of old who utters that which is more suitable for this age than his own:

The love of ʿAzza is nothing but the love of a beautiful woman
There are, in her absence, plenty of replacements

[171] What Ṣabrī means is that it can be accepted that your sexual desires are lessened with more interaction with women, but only on the condition that you actually fulfil those sexual desires properly in the first place, rather than simply being teased and left only with greater desire.

of security (i.e., in that men's nature will always pursue women to its natural end).

Its extent (i.e., the extent of what this claim of security presents) is that the eyes of modern men should become satiated by whatever they receive from them (i.e. women), and in retaining them. Rather, if it was possible for it to be stated, "satiated by what they obtained from them, by virtue of that which they did not obtain from them," then we would have considered it true security.[172]

So this is how the fallacies of the supporters of unveiling and mixed lifestyles break down [under scrutiny].

As for what the writer in the Turkish newspaper says, that "in this life is protection of chastity and satisfaction for the self (*nafs*)," then part of it is sufficient in contradicting the other [i.e., the latter part is sufficient in contradicting the former].[173]

As for the city man's narration about preventing his wife from [socialising with] the cook Tusun, the reason for that is that he considers him unsuitable to mix with the women in his class of people, and this "civilised" mixed lifestyle requires [mutual] suitability among its participants; they must know the [concocted] manners by which to exploit a woman's beauty and be open–in place of that–to being exploited themselves [by surrendering their *ghayra*], and neither of these two conditions are met in the cook Tusun.[174]

I do not accept the charge of breaking down these issues uncharitably, for that life certainly entails corruption unconducive to chastity, except that willful ignorance of those corruptions takes the place of chastity itself in that life, and those corruptions being compensated in kind is tolerated.[175]

---

[172] Meaning, what this lifestyle truly serves is male sexual gratification, and that will only come when men achieve what they want from the woman completely and then discard her for another. The only way that this philosophy would actually work, as mentioned by Ṣabrī, is if achieving some sexual gratification from seeing and playing with the woman (i.e., the preliminaries) were actually enough to satiate him and prevent him from seeking what it naturally entails of full sexual intercourse. Only in that case would this lifestyle be considered secure, but in fact, it is quite the opposite.

[173] Meaning, protecting chastity is incompatible with serving the desires of the *nafs*.

[174] What Ṣabrī is saying is that the man is not annoyed by his wife socialising with men, provided they are at his and her level, and would be similarly free with their own women.

[175] [Muṣṭafā Ṣabrī]: Many writers fault the Eastern poets of the past for their being excessively uninhibited and voicing obscenities in their love poems [riddled with eroticism]. I say: their licentiousness was mere imagination, difficult to consummate. However, blind imitation of the West in women's unveiling, and in their free-mixing with men, has caused these debaucheries to evolve from [mere] speech into actions; such that pursuing women has become something so ordinary that it is hardly worth mentioning!

Had we assumed that these modern garments for women, which are so revealing as to be more appropriate for a wedding chamber; and lewd free-mixing in these garments with strange men, dancing and twirling with them leg to leg, face to face, chest to chest; if we were to assume the impossible: that these preliminaries do not drag the two sexes towards the corruptions within themselves, it would still be a form of corruption in itself regardless.

Neither Islamic law nor a healthy disposition can accept strange men dispensing of [even] *some* of their lust using [part of] your wife's body, or that of your daughters' or sisters', nor that you should dispense of some of your lust using the bodies of their wives, daughters or sisters. Likewise, neither [Islamic law nor a healthy disposition] would accept that either of you dispense of [*all* your lust] with her [whole body] entirely.[176]

Our protectively jealous *Sharīʿa* deems even a single lewd touch between a man and a strange woman involving (*munṭawī*) lust as a form of marital relations between them, so it prohibits it for both progenitors, and progeny.[177]

Free-Mixing Among Western Youth

Let us hear now from an Egyptian columnist who studies in a Western university:

> "The system of free-mixing between young men and women at an early age is nonexistent in Egypt; there is almost no

[176] Abū Umāma reported: A young man came to the Prophet (ﷺ), and he said, "O Messenger of Allah, give me permission to commit adultery." The people turned to rebuke him, saying, "Quiet! Quiet!" The Prophet (ﷺ) said, "Come here." The young man came close and he told him to sit down. The Prophet (ﷺ) said, "Would you like that for your mother?" The man said, "No, by Allah, may I be sacrificed for you." The Prophet (ﷺ) said, "Neither would people like it for their mothers. Would you like that for your daughter?" The man said, "No, by Allah, may I be sacrificed for you." The Prophet (ﷺ) said, "Neither would people like it for their daughters. Would you like that for your sister?" The man said, "No, by Allah, may I be sacrificed for you." The Prophet (ﷺ) said, "Neither would people like it for their sisters. Would you like that for your aunts?" The man said, "No, by Allah, may I be sacrificed for you." The Prophet (ﷺ) said, "Neither would people like it for their aunts." Then, the Prophet (ﷺ) placed his hand on him and he said, "O Allah, forgive his sins, purify his heart, and guard his chastity." After that, the young man never again inclined toward anything sinful. See: *Musnad Aḥmad* (22211).

[177] In the Dār al-Lubāb edition, Muḥammad Wā'il al-Ḥanbalī, states: Imām Abū Ḥanīfa (may Allāh have mercy on him) considered the mere touching of a woman with sexual desire to prohibit [any possible valid] marital relations with her progenitors and her progeny. Other scholars differed with him on this. See: Ṣabrī (n. 70), at 83 fn.1., *al-Mawsūʿa al-Fiqhiyya al-Kuwaytiyya.* 2nd ed. Vol. 37. 45 vols. Kuwait: Wizārat al-Awqāf wa 'l-Shu'ūn al-Islāmiyya–al-Kuwayt, 2006, 37/284.

trace of it, except in some of our aristocratic families who have lived a long time in Europe.

As for Egypt, the young man and woman remain completely separated from their childhood; conversation is prohibited even between young boys and girls of the same family, and they legitimise this prohibition of theirs by [highlighting] that this barrier established between them prevents that which could occur [as a result of] the desires of adolescence. If they [seriously] considered this for a long time, they would realise that they are gravely mistaken, and the result is the opposite of what they intend. For in this state every single one of them maintains communication with their friend not as innocent friendship, but rather seeking sexual relations, for which their free-mixing was prohibited in the first place. It is as though they shatter that barrier to pieces as revenge on their families.

What is more, [consider] the elaborate scheming and planning the two must think up in order to reach one another. [Consider] how they attempt this by hidden means, such that no one even realises what is happening behind drawn curtains. This deep thought, [planning and colluding], only hurts them both.

You'll find, for example, a young man despondent during [his] lecture at school; perhaps the teacher is explaining a theory in engineering while he daydreams about the scheduled time to meet her [i.e. his female friend], and the same is the case with the girl. [Consider] how much this type of thinking and mentality really leaves its trace in our sensitive society! And this disease of hysteria which strikes many of our young girls during puberty is itself nothing but a result of this [mentality].[178]

So if these barriers, propped up by fathers, were to be removed, and strong manners instilled in the souls of these young men and women, and they grew up from a young age in a mixed environment, that untamed emotion would weaken with time, and good companionship would strengthen by contrast, going no further than innocent interests and free-mixing which awakens a

---

[178] The concept of hysteria as a medical disorder, considered especially prevalent among women, was widespread in the late 19th and early 20th centuries. For more on the sociological history of hysteria, see: Tasca C, Rapetti M, Carta MG, Fadda B. Women and hysteria in the history of mental health. *Clin Pract Epidemiol Ment Health.* 2012;8:110-9. Last Accessed: December 15th, 2023.
https://www.ncbi.nlm.nih.gov/pmc/articles/PMC3480686/.

love of beauty in the heart; because it is only beauty, after all–not filth and the degradation of oneself into a cheap commodity.[179]

And we often read in our local newspapers about the daughters of some families running away with the servants [of that home], answering the call of emotion. And these extreme laws and what these family systems force upon their [innocent] virgin girls? They only aggravate those [emotions].

The system of free-mixing in English families, [on the other hand], pleases me very much. You see a young boy accompanying the neighbour's young girl, playing together in the garden of one of their homes, and they remain like that until their adolescence. He progresses from playing with her to being her colleague in education. Both then invite the other to tea [outside of school]. How happy are the parents when their son or daughter informs them that he or she will spend their day with their friend! They welcome their boy's [female] friend, displaying all sorts of emotion and fondness to her in a manner that would make him happy, raise her boyfriend in her eyes, and give him complete respect. She accompanies him in his higher education at university, and that is a splendid companionship. He reviews his lecture notes with her, they try to understand it together, and they become aides to one another. He benefits from her preciseness in work–a trait of the fairer sex, and she benefits from him through that with which man has been naturally endowed–patience through hardships and bearing difficulty with a smile. Each benefits from the other, and they graduate at year's end each holding tight the hand of their colleague, each congratulating the other of success.

The reason for the English students being ahead, despite the difficulties of university and the burdens of work, is simple: if we were to know about his affairs and came to grasp even a little of his internal life, we would find that he is no smarter than the Egyptian in anything, nor has he been created from a substance any different than the Egyptian. [The difference is that] his thoughts are confined to his work, and not in meeting with his

[179] The author means, if young people were accustomed to mixed interactions, they would not chase after boyfriends and girlfriends like a degrading, cheap commodity.

young girl or how to flirt with her. He doesn't think about that while she's next to him in a lecture, or in the workplace. She smiles innocently to him whenever their eyes meet, then each returns to completing their work, with earnest energy."

– Muḥammad Ḥāmid Shākir
Department of Physiology – Liverpool University

The student columnist addresses his people, guiding them to the methodology of social development (*tarbiyya*) he noticed in the West. He prefers that [Western] social order without giving the least glance or consideration for the religion of his people, or the manners of his fathers and forefathers, or [the fact] that the readers of his published column in *al-Ahrām* under the title "Effects of the Environment in Society" have not yet lost–or at least some among them have not yet lost–sound judgement and reasoning.

Could the columnist first and foremost guarantee them [i.e., the readers of his article] that the system of free-mixing between the young man and woman to which he alludes, especially in some aristocratic Egyptian families which have lived a long time in Europe, has [actually] been beneficial for them and left any positive effects?

On top of that, the student columnist is well-aware of what comes from the mixing of the two sexes, which he calls an 'innocent' friendship, or an 'innocent' tendency or an 'innocent' smile–and naturally, 'innocent' hugging and embracing would be added to that as well, because the male and female classmate raised with the manners of Western civilisation must on some occasions dance together. All of these innocent acts, along with the beauty they awaken in the heart, because it is 'only beauty' as the writer says; these are but deceitful titles and descriptions. They are employed to deceive the naïve, and act as an affront to human modesty under the curtain of innocent words used outside of their context. [This is] similar to how some thieves steal with their faces [hidden] under a cover. [These deceptions are similar to] how the callers to unveiling term themselves 'advocates of women,' and term the callers to veiling as her 'enemies.' Allāh knows best who are the true advocates and the true enemies, just as He knows the corrupt from those who call to righteousness.[180]

---

[180] This expression is borrowed from the Qur'ānic verse, "...And Allah knows who intends harm and who intends good..." [*al-Baqara*: 220] One might note that the obfuscation of terms remains a prevalent tool of

Look also to what the columnist says regarding the placement of a veil between the young man and woman, "For in this state every single one of them maintains communication with their friend not as innocent friendship, but rather seeking sexual relations, for which their free-mixing was prohibited in the first place." It is as though their sexuality disappears when you allow free-mixing between them; as though both turn into men or both turn into women!

On top of that, why would his communication with his female friend remain innocent when free-mixing is allowed, and *not* innocent when it is prohibited?! If corruption [supposedly] arises from the prohibition, as will be soon discussed, rather than from the natural disposition of the free-mixers, then there is no doubt that permitting free-mixing also [seeks to] prevent non-innocent contact. [Thus, in communicating in that manner] he would necessarily be doing something he was prohibited from [in the first place, and not because of his natural inclination towards such].[181]

[The columnist also mentions,] "It is as though they shatter that barrier to pieces as revenge on their families."

This is similar to the statement that, "a man is compelled towards doing that which is prohibited." It is as though, were they not prevented from reaching out to one another and there was no barrier placed between them, they would not have pounced upon this prohibited communication.

Based upon that: certainly, the claims of those calling for unveiling would then entail that the veil (*ḥijāb*) compels [one towards] temptation the most. The veil would [additionally] comprise [all the aforementioned forms of] corruption which the premise of unveiling and the facilitation of free-mixing seeks to restrict.

One may, in fact, hear this kind of talk from them [i.e., its supporters], but it is all sophistry and misguidance. For if it were the case that an action's prevention leads to the action's occurrence more than if it were left permissible, then the whole matter of command and prohibition

---

those who call for sexual libertinism. For example, it is often not enough today to remain silent on matters related to sexual attraction and gender, rather, one must be an 'ally' to be considered a positive member of 'civilised' society.

[181] What Ṣabrī means, as he will soon further clarify, is that both those who prohibit free-mixing and those who facilitate it both seek, according to their own methods, to prevent adultery. Ṣabrī's response is that, in either case, if couples engage in adultery, they are necessarily doing something prohibited. Someone dead-set on sinning in this way will do so despite the rules on its preliminaries, such as free-mixing.

(*al-amr wa 'l-nahī*)[182] would be upended and reversed; as the barrier would become a path, and the path a barrier! It would necessitate shutting down all the laws of punishment in the world, because their end result among criminals would be the encouragement and promotion of the crime itself,[183] as revenge upon those who instituted the laws in the first place![184]

Had the columnist instead said that, "[they are] taking advantage of an opportunity that doesn't often come with the preventative veil,"[185] that would have more closely resembled the truth. If there had been no veil between them, and all of them could mix and communicate with one another as they wished, then they would have all the time [in the world to do so], and there would be no need to rush because all of that time would be [open] opportunities.

I remembered here a story, one which I won't continue without presenting:

> "There was a man travelling together with a non-related woman (*ajnabiyya*). The man says to her, "do you know what will happen when we pass beyond this mountain?" She responds: "what will happen?" He says, "I will assault you there. You will refuse, and reject my advance. You will cry loudly and [try to] seek help without finding any. There will occur between us a violent altercation, the end of which none can predict." So the woman listened, then said "nothing which you have feared from me will

---

[182] The Islamic principle of *amr bi l-ma'rūf wa nahy 'an al-munkar* dictates that Muslims must enjoin what is good and prohibit what is evil. For more on the topic, please see: Cook, Michael. *Commanding Right and Forbidding Wrong in Islamic Thought.* Cambridge: Cambridge University Press, 2001.

[183] Following similarly flawed logic, many today call for the decriminalisation of marijuana, as well as other drugs and narcotics. Others call for the decriminalisation of prostitution where it remains illegal. Some even go so far as to call for the defunding and disestablishment of their local police force altogether, believing that permissiveness and facilitation would better prevent the harmful effects of drug-use, prostitution, and their like.

[184] Many Muslims today call for leniency against blasphemy laws present in the Muslim world. They believe that harsh reactions against those mocking the Prophet (ﷺ) only lead to further ridicule and bad press for Muslims. They forget, however, that if Muslim societies were to replicate the same forms of leniency, this would lead toward depictions of the Prophet (ﷺ) similar to how modern Western societies often depict Jesus Christ (peace be upon him) in popular culture and media: with mockery, sarcasm, and ridicule.

[185] What Ṣabrī means is that, had the writer said that youth rushing to meet each other in a restricted society is simply an example of them taking advantage of a rare opportunity, rather than trying to spite the elders, that would have made more sense.

happen, because I will comply with what you want from me, and the matter will be sorted peacefully."[186]

We return to the columnist's statement, "What is more, [consider] the elaborate scheming and planning the two must think up in order to reach one another."

This is a waste of time and energy for both of them, while possibly making the matter (of supervision and surveillance) easier for their parents.[187]

The columnist also says, "...they attempt that in hidden ways, such that no one even realises what is happening behind drawn curtains."

This despite the fact that open disclosure (*al-mujāhara*)[188] is preferable to secrecy. It is more indicative of braveness and more reflective of freedom.[189]

He continues, "This deep thought, [planning and colluding], only hurts them both. You'll find, for example, a young man despondent during [his] lecture at school...."

If his girl was always within reach, beside him, in his eyes, he would be crisp, joyous and energetic (*hashshan bashshan*) at all times. If the columnist was someone who actually prayed in mosques, perhaps he would have hoped–if only he could pray next to beautiful young girls in the same row. Or perhaps he could pray while they were in front of him in the row ahead such that they (i.e., their rears) would appear to him like [voluptuous] new moons (*ahilla*) when they bowed down (in *rukūʿ*), and their backs like slender tree branches while they stood! Perhaps he would find pleasure in prayer as he has never before found in mosques packed merely with men.

---

[186] Ṣabrī mentions this anecdote here to suggest that the idea of men being untamed and the subsequent debate on veiling and free-mixing being a means by which to manage such behaviour misses the mark in the first place. This is because women desire men all the same, and immorality is not prevalent because men are necessarily more exhibited and predatorial, but rather because humans, both men and women, are of sexual nature, compelled towards the fulfillment of their carnal desires with each other.

[187] What Ṣabrī means here is that, at the very least, prohibition makes things difficult for the youth and easy for their parents to control and monitor, as compared with making everything open, whereby it becomes much easier for them to engage in the same immoral actions which would otherwise have required planning and risk.

[188] The Prophet (ﷺ) said that the sin committed openly and without shame (*mujāhara*) cannot be forgiven. Abū Hurayra narrates, "All the people of my nation will be pardoned for their sins except those who publicise them..." See: *Ṣaḥīḥ al-Bukhārī* (6069) Chapter: A Believer Conceals His Sins, *Ṣaḥīḥ Muslim* (2990) Chapter: The Prohibition Against Disclosing One's Own Sins.

[189] Ṣabrī is being sarcastic throughout this entire response.

Perhaps [this arrangement] would make young men who run from prayer [instead] tie themselves to the mosques.[190]

The columnist also says, "perhaps the teacher is explaining a theory in engineering while he daydreams about the scheduled time to meet her [i.e., his female friend]..." If the barrier were lifted and free-mixing permitted, then [we are led to conclude that] the student's mind would remain present with him everywhere, as would the [mind of] the one he [actually] seeks [i.e. his female friend].

He continues, "and the same is the case with the girl. [Consider] how much this type of thinking and mentality leaves its trace in our sensitive society! This disease of hysteria which strikes many of our young girls during puberty is itself nothing but a result of this [mentality]."

Our poor girls! They are plagued by their deprivation of young men to entertain them, to accompany them in school, in houses, in streets, and parks; if only they could inhale freedom and love with them!

The columnist says, "We often read in our local newspapers about the daughters of some families running away with the servants [of that home], answering the call of emotion. And these extreme laws and what these family systems force upon their [innocent] virgin girls? They only aggravate those [emotions]."

If the columnist possessed even a distant relationship with the discipline of logic, he would have noted the fact that those Egyptian girls running away with their servants was a result *of* free-mixing between man and woman, which we warn against, and to which he calls. Occurrences of this type should not be counted as a sin and blemish upon the family laws which prevent the mixing of the sexes. Should the servant not be counted among males, or among the non-related?[191] Or should the girl not be considered among the females? She, as the columnist loves, was raised with the servant's company and would see him every day. If *their* free-mixing was sufficient to lure her (*ighwā'*), what would you think of her mixing with a young man of her own social class? Such occurrences reveal the fallacy of his claim, while he mentions them in order to support it!

What is necessary for Egyptian (and non-Egyptian) parents is to test the level of their children's healthy intellect and understanding before sending them to Western schools. If [they do] not, then perhaps there would be nothing to prevent them one day from writing letters [while abroad] to

[190] Many Muslim institutions today relax free-mixing norms under similar pretences of bringing the youth to practising environments and the mosque.

[191] i.e., an unrelated male prohibited from socialising with the family's women in Islamic law.

Egyptian newspapers, openly and explicitly calling their fathers and brothers to the religion of the Westerners which they consider to be true based upon their intellects. We have shown you some distorted examples of their thought.

The Western Colonisation of the Minds of Our Youth is Worse than Their Colonisation of Our Lands

In concluding my response to the university student's column, I say: Egyptians can only dream of the independence of their nation, because the West has already colonised the hearts of their educated children! And colonisation of the heart is the strongest form of occupation, and the most dangerous and capable of annihilating nations out of existence.

Education that Guarantees the Virtues of Women

Among the statements of those who call to unveiling, with which they distort their falsehoods, and present them as truth, is:

> "Indeed the guarantee of virtue (*'iffa*) in women–which must be maintained–is [achieved through] their education and advancement, to build intellectual strength within her and cultivate her, and to make it–that is, intellectual strength–control the lower self. It is through knowledge and advancement that a young girl's virtue is determined, and limited by that [in relation to what she lacks of it] too. She becomes gravely weakened if she is veiled and kept in a world disconnected from that of men."[192]

We do not dispute the fact that [virtue is] a notable trait within the young girl which she might use to control her lower self, and which depends on education and cultivation. Rather, what we do dispute is that she should be considered free from and in no need of wearing the *ḥijāb*, which Islam has mandated upon her, because of [education]. This is because, just as we know that 'self-control' is not found in abundance among our acquaintances–well-educated and cultivated men–we also cannot guarantee [safety] from our present affliction when we place such men of 'self-control' before the

---

[192] Ṣabrī is implying that the influences to which one is exposed in early life can last a lifetime, whether acclimating a woman to everyday contact with unrelated men, or to being isolated from them.

magnetic attraction buried deep in a woman's beauty. It is likewise the case when we place our 'self-controlled' women and girls face-to-face with the lure of those human devils,[193] especially those modern-day men equipped with advanced techniques [of deception, hustling].

The inability to control oneself among either of the sexes is sufficient to create discord (*fitna*) when they free-mix, so we fear for each from the other, and we cannot reject these doubts which surround us, even if others may reject [their existence], because maintaining self-control is something easy to say, but difficult to do.

What more can we say about this than what our master [Prophet] Yūsuf (peace be upon him) said, "I do not seek to free myself from blame, for indeed the soul is ever inclined to evil." [*Yūsuf*: 53][194]

To summarise: Certainly, control over the lower self, whether present or absent, and its level of sufficiency and [ability] to resist [urges] is something that cannot be quantified. Its [true] nature is hidden within everyone, such that no other person is acquainted with it. Rather, how often does someone err in their estimation of *themselves* in those dangerous and delicate situations?

How perfect is the statement of *al-Sharīf* al-Raḍī (d. 406/1015)[195] who said:

> *Virtue is not virtuous when those situations are in control*
> *of its core; nor is the trustworthy to be trusted.*[196]

[This is] especially so given the fact that the level of virtue for one who has not learned of its religious obligation, or even deduced it

---

[193] In Islamic belief, a devil or demon (*shayṭān*) can be a jinn or a human being. A demonic human is simply an exceptionally evil and malevolent individual. However, Ṣabrī is likely speaking figuratively in this sentence, not saying that corrupt men are literal devils.

[194] This verse is part of the incident in which the wife of a wealthy Egyptian official attempts to seduce Yūsuf (known as Joseph, son of Isaac in the Bible), losing her self-control due to his stunningly attractive appearance.

[195] Abū 'l-Ḥasan Muḥammad b. al-Ḥusayn al-Mūsawī, better known as al-Sharīf al-Raḍī, was a Shīʿī scholar, author and poet of 10th and 11th century Iraq. He was born in Abbasid Baghdad to an affluent Shīʿī family descended from the seventh Twelver Imām. He studied under the famous Twelver theologian Shaykh al-Mufīd. By far his most famous work was the compilation of *Nahj al-Balāgha,* a collection of sermons, epistles, and sayings of the Prophet's nephew (and first Imām in Twelver theology), 'Alī b. Abī Ṭālib. The work is considered a masterpiece of Shīʿī literature, although critics have called into question how much of its content is authentic, and how much al-Raḍī's own writings.

[196] What al-Raḍī means is that there is no virtue in remaining virtuous and honourable in situations which do not test one's virtue; one's mettle is only known when tested. See: Sharīf al-Raḍī, Muḥammad b. al-Ḥusayn al-. *Dīwān al-Sharīf al-Raḍī.* 1st ed. Vol. 2. 2 vols. Tehran, Iran: Manshūrāt Maṭba'a Wizārat al-Irshād al-Islāmī., 1986, 2/471.

intellectually, does not pass beyond [the intention] that people should simply perceive him as virtuous, and that his image be preserved amongst them, which is not real virtue at all. So no matter how virtuous someone is known to be, and no matter how complete the mind or inviolate one's intellectual discernment, it may still be insufficient in such [tempting] situations which are natural pitfalls for anyone.

Given that, it is necessary that the soul should be denied even the first opportunity [to stray], and that its paths be blocked. **The [true] meaning of the woman's veil is to close off the lower self's paths of opportunity as concisely as possible.**

One Turkish writer–who supports unveiling–scorns the strength of those light silken *burqa*s on the faces of those women, while simultaneously admitting that those *burqa*s make the woman as though living in another world. So I said to him that this is, in fact, an admission from you of its strength; those light veils that serve as curtains of modesty placed between the sexes, preventing one from mixing with the other, limit a man's communication [with women], [so much so that they] even [limit his communication] with his wife outside their home, and make [that communication] even less than what one would see in the lands of Western civilisation.

I saw often enough with my own two eyes on the streets of Paris,[197] a man walking and holding a woman's hand, speaking to and kissing her within sight and earshot of those passing by. This woman is not necessarily his wife either. This is the state of those lands, which the proponents of unveiling claim are free of corrupting influences; and many heedless people vouch for this claim of theirs, as though these were innocent kisses!! Perhaps you may find evidence for the innocence of such acts by pointing out that they occur in open daylight!![198]

Unveiling in its Modern Conception is Rejected by Islam

[197] Ṣabrī's first migration, nearly avoiding a raid on his home by the İttihad ve Terakki Cemiyeti (Committee for Unity and Progress, or CUP) regime, was to Egypt in 1913. From there, he travelled to Bosnia, then Paris, and eventually settled in Bucharest until the First World War, after which he would return to Turkey once more. See: Gharad (n. 11), at 137.

[198] That is, one might suppose that a practice being socially acceptable in public during the day, such as kissing in a city like Paris, is evidence of its moral acceptability, but this is a false conclusion, says Ṣabrī. Just because an illicit practice is no longer kept hidden from the public eye is not evidence of its acceptability in the eyes of Allāh.

Furthermore, everyone knows that Islam rejects unveiling according to its modern meaning which we have clarified. Despite that, you will see many writers with Muslim names calling towards it, encouraging Muslim women to it [as well], and they fall upon those who contradict them with curses. They consider them to be backwards; people whose statements and disagreements should not even be considered [or debated]. At least they [the opponents of unveiling] continue debating those with whom they disagree.

For example, you may see the writer of "*In Summary*" in the *al-Ahrām* newspaper–whose name is Aḥmad–who, while lauding Christmas, clarifies that he is a Muslim, a believer in Muḥammad (ﷺ) and in our master 'Īsā (peace be upon him) who spoke in the cradle as an infant, and who said, "Indeed, I am a slave of Allāh, He gave me the Book, and made me a Prophet, and made me a blessing wherever I go." [*Maryam*: 30-31] You see this same person time and again aiming arrows of disdain and ridicule at those scholars and writers displeased with the Muslim woman's unveiling.

Does he not understand that the [so-called] 'backwardness' he faults in his opponents, is in fact a going 'backwards' towards Islam? And that he, with these foul, ribald arrows, shoots at the religion of Islam and its Book, which explicitly mentions that women "should draw their veils over their chests, and not reveal their [hidden] adornments except to their husbands, fathers, fathers-in-law, sons, stepsons, brothers, their brothers' sons or sisters' sons, their fellow women, those 'bondswomen' [i.e. slaves] in their possession, male attendants with no desire, or children still unaware of women's nakedness. Let them not stomp their feet, drawing attention to their hidden adornments." [*al-Nūr*: 31]

If you were to ask him: what does he say about the text of the Qur'ān and the great care and concern it gives to [highlighting and annotating the matter with] such sublime details? He will not hesitate to reply, as though flabbergasted [by such an obvious question], and his demeanour would echo, "Certainly, he who lives in the twentieth century and relies on the Qur'ān for his social views, then responding to him is entirely [futile and] stupid!" He does not even see that you should rightly be astonished at him, seeing as he is a 'cultured' Muslim. How is it that when it comes to the issue of women, he goes around and around in his writings, all while remaining ignorant of the longest verse in the Book of Islam pertaining to women?![199] Even if you read it to him, he would turn his back and flee as though he had not heard it,[200] and he would compensate you for your trouble of teaching it to him by considering you as someone unworthy of even speaking to [anymore], so how, pray tell, has he learned?! How is he even Muslim when he believes in the Qur'ānic verses he wants, and does not believe in others, nor does he see it being worthy as proof for those who seek it?![201]

Apart from the verse of the *ḥijāb*, there are many prophetic narrations which command covering women from non-related men, and which prohibit mixing with them. However, the writer and his ilk do not heed the verses or prophetic narrations which contradict the customs of Western civilisation, no matter how disgraceful the result. It is as though they were messengers (*rusul*)[202] of that civilisation in the East after the messengers of Allāh, their revelation abrogating the revelation that came before them![203] This is despite the contradiction of these modern messengers with the [true] Messengers of Allāh,[204] and their secretly waging war against them. They are [only] Muslims and believers in Allāh and His messengers if

---

[199] Someone who selectively chooses some Qur'ānic verses and *aḥādīth* (pl. of ḥadīth) to make a point, while ignoring others which contradict that point might be accused of having made up their mind at the outset, and then searching for evidence afterwards to justify it.

[200] This is borrowed from the Qur'ān, "Whenever Our revelations are recited to them, they turn away in arrogance as if they did not hear them, as if there is deafness in their ears. So give them good news ⌜O Prophet⌝ of a painful punishment." [*Luqmān*: 7]

[201] Meaning, how can he be a Muslim when he does not accept the Qur'ān as a valid proof from which to derive conclusions and legislation. The Qur'ān similarly criticises the Jews for selectively choosing from their divine scripture. "...Do you believe in some of the Scripture and reject the rest? Is there any reward for those who do so among you other than disgrace in this worldly life and being subjected to the harshest punishment on the Day of Judgment?..." [*al-Baqara*: 85]

[202] The word *rusul* is much more evocative in Arabic than English. In Arabic, a Messenger (*rasūl*, pl. of *rusul*) is the bearer of divine revelation from Allāh for mankind. The Prophet Muḥammad (ﷺ) is often described honourifically as the Messenger of Allāh (*Rasūl Allāh*).

[203] Islamic creed holds that revelation is progressive, beginning with the first Prophet Ādam (peace be upon him) and terminating with the final Prophet, Muḥammad (ﷺ). A series of Prophets were chosen by Allāh to be bearers of revelation and laws to guide mankind, each abrogating the authority of the last. Moses and Jesus (*alayhimā 'l-salām*) are among the Prophets sent with laws for their own communities, but they, and all others were finally abrogated by the law of Islam sent with Muḥammad (ﷺ). Even in the law of Islam, the *sharī'a* was revealed progressively over the 23 years of the Qur'ān's revelation. Certain things which were licit in the earliest years of Islam were made illicit through the process of abrogation (*naskh*). Ṣabrī's suggestion that some Muslims infatuated with the West consider themselves as prophets abrogating the message of Islam implicitly suggests that they have taken the worldview of Western civilisation as a new religion in place of Islam, or at least are insincere in their adherence to Islam.

[204] The messages of the prophets affirm one another; the messages of these false messengers contradict their predecessors.

the call of faith and Islam was in concordance with the destruction of its basic characteristics.[205]

People in this strange day and age do not care to point out the enemies of Islam hiding under Muslim names, who seek to achieve through [subterfuge] in their homelands what writers from outside of and unaffiliated with the Muslim world (*umma*) could not achieve, due to the ease with which the former can guide towards [corruption] under the sheltering protection of names, and the ease with which people will listen to them.[206]

In Egypt there are writers Muslim by name and claim, but who [have in fact] left the religion of their people. The Muslim world [initially] stood up against them, but [ultimately] did not remain [as such], considering them repentant. It [not only] returned them to its enclosure, but submitted its reigns [of leadership] to them [as well]. If they did not have their [Muslim] names as intercession[207] it would not have been easy for them to pose as penitents, nor would people have accepted their repentance. Were people as worried over their religion as they are over their wealth, they would have been cautious against allowing them to return to their refuge.

Allāh may Forgive the Unveiling Woman, but the Advocates of Unveiling Are Removed from Islam

It cannot be argued against me that the Muslim makes mistakes and commits a sin, or sins rather, and the position of orthodox Sunni Islam (the *Ahl al-Sunna*) is that major sins do not expel a person from the religion; such as this cannot be used to argue against me, for disobedience to Allāh and His Messenger in speech cannot be equated to disobedience to them in

---

[205] [Muṣṭafā Ṣabrī]: As for the Turkish writer Jalāl Nūrī (Celal Nuri), see what he says in some of his writings: "Indeed, who enters into the religion of Islam does not exit it, for in it is circumcision." What Ṣabrī may mean here is that Muslims, even if totally lacking in faith, are assumed to be Muslims due to the circumstances of their lives, such as being from Muslim families and being circumcised.

[206] What Ṣabrī means is that people of Muslim backgrounds who advocate for unveiling, free-mixing and so on can influence Muslims more easily than non-Muslims, as they are culturally familiar with their audiences and can pose as orthodox Muslims when it suits them. This is well-understood by non-Muslims who seek to influence the religion today, as exemplified in the infamous RAND report *Building Moderate Muslim Networks*, which calls for the US government to broadly support liberal and reformist figures in the Muslim world. See: Rabasa, Angela, Cheryl Benard, Lowell H. Schwartz, and Peter Sickle. *Building Moderate Muslim Networks*. Center for Middle East Public Policy. Arlington, Virginia: RAND Corporation, 2007. Last Accessed: December 15, 2023. https://www.rand.org/content/dam/rand/pubs/monographs/2007/RAND_MG574.pdf.

[207] Meaning, if their names did not make them appear to be Muslim, they would have had a harder time advancing their agenda.

action.[208] It is not possible for a Muslim to contradict Allāh and His Messenger in his speech and statements, even if it is possible that his actions may not be in accordance with what Allāh and His Messenger have commanded.

Let us mention an example of this pertinent to our subject [at hand]: if a Muslim woman was to unveil in the modern sense of the word, and participate in some soirées with a dress that does not properly cover her, or even live her whole life in this state of modern unveiling, going along with what it necessitates of the different forms of unveiling and free-mixing, and following in all of that her internal desires; it is possible for this woman to remain upon her Islam, even if her continuing upon [this life] severely weakens the prospect of her remaining Muslim![209] So this sinful *act* is not considered in itself an abandonment of the religion, and [not only that, but because] it is driven along by her innate sexuality; so perhaps Allāh can forgive her. Likewise is the state of the man who mixes with her, and who–indeed–benefits from her unveiling, [Allāh may forgive him too].

As for repudiation of the explicit Qur'ānic [text] which commands the covering of women, then that is worse than the action [of unveiling] itself, and it is sufficient for the one who utters it [in contradiction to the Qur'ānic edict] to have abandoned Islam, as there is no natural drive [for one to utter that] other than a lack of faith in the Qur'ān [itself].

Muslim Governments Should No Longer Register Heretics as Muslims

Unveiling is not something that can be called towards or defended by a Muslim writer in a Muslim country like Egypt. Because of that, my final statement for those calling to it and defending it is that logic, good character, and valor enjoin them to cease their call and defence, or [otherwise] cease to claim that they are Muslims, if only by name.

---

[208] Mainstream Sunni theologians hold that sinners are not to be excommunicated from the faith. To excommunicate people based on sins, even major ones, is considered heresy; a hallmark of the heterodox Khārijī sect heavily censured by early scholars. This is different, as Ṣabrī indicates, than the one who vocally contradicts the foundational Islamic source texts (the Qur'ān and the Sunna) themselves. This latter type would be classified as a *jāḥid* (an obstinate denier) or a *mustaḥill* (someone who holds something permissible that is otherwise prohibited in said texts). In both cases, this rejection would be tantamount to disbelief in the texts themselves, as opposed to a mere sin, and could thus potentially expel one from the faith.

[209] Ṣabrī seems to suggest that faith (*īmān*) increases and decreases, rather than existing as a binary opposite of disbelief. This is concurrent with mainstream Sunnī theological doctrine. See: Ibn Abī Ya'lā, Muḥammad. *Ṭabaqāt al-Ḥanābila*. Cairo, Egypt: Maṭba'a al-Sunna al-Muḥammadiyya, 1952, 1/130-131.

The time has come for Muslim governments to, at the very least, stop the heretics advancing in their lands from being counted among the ranks of Muslims, if they cannot deal with them as the apostates that they are.[210]

Yes! Perhaps it is appropriate for unveiling to be advocated in countries which have explicitly dissociated themselves from their religion, such as modern Turkey (Türkiye).

And although I have considered actions to be less evil than words as they pertain to sins (such as unveiling), I make an exception for what I have read in an article dedicated to Sa'd [Zaghlūl]. For it was he himself who unveiled women by his own hand in a gathering with their husbands [present], and that was counted among his virtues! [I make an exception in this case] because the action of a great leader such as Sa'd is considered like legislation by his partisans, and as education by his supporters. However, [similar to speech as described earlier] there is no natural drive for this legislation and education, so that action [similar to speech] will not be forgiven for him; in fact, it would be considered to fall under [the ruling on] speech and command.[211] [212]

[It is as if] I can see them now, the religious scholars who kept silent when that event [i.e. the mass-unveiling][213] happened, out of respect for Sa'd, or the few who criticised him without explicitly mentioning his

---

[210] The general punishment for apostasy in Islamic law is death, though ascertaining apostasy can often be a burdensome task.

[211] That is, commanding something with the authority or power to see that command carried out can be considered like an action in the law. Consider the example of someone who wields enormous leverage over someone else, and commands him to commit an illegal act; the one who commands it would bear some responsibility for the crime.

[212] Muḥammad Wā'il al-Ḥanbalī notes with surprise that al-Ziriklī (d. 1976) mentioned him [Sa'd] in *al-A'lām* with words of praise and honour. See: Ṣabrī (n. 70), at 96 fn. 2., al-Ziriklī, Khayr al-Dīn. *al-A'lām* 15th ed. Vol. 3. 8 vols. Beirut, Lebanon: Dār al-'Ilm li 'l-Malāyīn, 2002, 3/83.

[213] Though debated, some historians note this incident as having occurred during the 1919 Egyptian Revolution. Several feminist leaders, including Hudā Sha'rāwī, removed their veils at Tahrir Square and when Sa'd Zaghlūl came, he himself removed the veils of those awaiting his arrival. Muhammad Ali Attasi notes that, "...in her book, "Veiling and Unveiling," Natheera Zein al-Din quotes the literary writer, May Zeyadeh, who remarked of this incident in the Egyptian newspaper, *Al-Ahram*: 'Is there a more significant factor affecting women's unveiling than the actions of the leader [Zaghlūl] upon his appearance at the women's congregation waiting there to welcome him? Indeed, his hand was faster than his mouth in expressing his wish, when, laughing, he reached over and removed the veil from the face of the woman demonstrator who was standing closest to him. His action was received with applause and ululations. The women there followed suit and took off their veils, signalling in that day, the liberation of women.'" See: Atassi, Muhammad Ali. "The Veiling of the City." *Al Jadid* 16, no. 62 (2010). Last Accessed: December 15th, 2023. https://www.aljadid.com/content/veiling-city.

name, as is custom of criticism among the scholars of Egypt.[214] However, forbidding evil is not a struggle (*jihād*) against thin air, and indeed the truth and the spirit of Islam is greater than Saʿd, or a thousand Saʿds. I would draw your attention here to the companion Sa'd and what the Prophet (ﷺ) said to him, "You all are astonished by the protective jealousy (*ghayra*) of Sa'd! By Allāh, I am more protectively jealous than him, and Allāh is more protectively jealous than me."[215]

The Ḥijāb Does not Prevent Prosperity; Islam Does not Prevent Women's Education

They may say, "The unveiling of women is certainly an intrinsic part of the Renaissance (*Nahḍa*)[216] which the Muslims need, and that is why Saʿd implemented it!"

To which I respond: the age in which the 'renaissance' of the Muslims reached its [true] peak was undoubtedly the age of our master 'Umar al-Fārūq.[217] No nation at any period has reached the level of that renaissance, and the world will never again see anything like the Muslims' glorious feats of that golden age. Nevertheless, the very first of those who spoke of the mandate of *ḥijāb* for women was 'Umar. Then the Qur'ān

---

[214] The famous Egyptian journalist and poet 'Abbās al-'Aqqād (d. 1383/1964) wrote that "Sa'd Zaghlūl was a man whose views on womanhood and the proper behaviour of a spouse contradicted the view of the overwhelming majority in those times, as in all times. It is sufficient to know that he was the one who aided Qāsim Amīn, his colleague and close friend, in popularising his work *The Liberation of Women*, and encouraged him to bear the backlash and strife he received as a result." See: 'Aqqād, 'Abbās Maḥmūd al-. *Sa'd Zaghlūl: Ṣīra wa Taḥiyya*. Cairo, Egypt: Maṭbaʿa Ḥijāzī bi 'l-Qāhira, 1936.

[215] Ṣabrī here refers to the Companion Sa'd b. 'Ubāda (may Allāh be pleased with him). It was stated that he only married virgins, and no one would dare marry any woman he had divorced, even after their waiting period. When asked what he would do if he found another man with his wife, he responded "I would behead him with the blade of my sword." See: *Ṣaḥīḥ al-Bukhārī* (7416) Chapter: No One Has More Ghayra than Allāh.

[216] The Arab Renaissance (*al-nahḍat al-'arabiyya*) was a wide-ranging cultural and political movement conventionally dated to span the mid-19th to early 20th century, concentrated mainly in Egypt. The Nahḍa era saw the rise of Arab nationalism, the spread of new technologies such as the printing press and railway, and the genesis of modern Arabic literature, among other developments. Although Nahḍa-era writers, activists, artists, religious scholars and scientists varied widely in ideological orientation, it can be said that the common aspiration of all was to see the Arab world return to the cultural and political vitality which characterised the classical age of Islamic history. Many writers of the Nahḍa period argued for extensive imitation of Europe not only in science and technology, but in social mores as well. It is this group to whom Ṣabrī is referring here. For more on the Nahḍa, its precedents and legacy in the Arab world, see: Shilaq, Aḥmad Zakariyyā al-. *Min al-nahḍa ilā al-istināra: fī tārīkh al-fikr al-Miṣrī al-ḥadīth*. First printing. Cairo, Egypt: Dār al-Karma, 2022.

[217] 'Umar b. al-Khaṭṭāb (may Allāh be pleased with him), the second Caliph of Islam who reigned over a vast and united Islamic empire from 634 to 644 AD.

revealed [verses] in accordance with his position, may Allāh be pleased with him.[218]

Reflect on this, and upon the difference between the *ḥijāb* being decreed after it did not exist, and then it being lifted after it remained practised throughout Islamic history. And [having done so], finally reflect upon what our master Abū Bakr al-Ṣiddīq,[219] may Allāh be pleased with him, said, "The affairs of the last [generations] of this nation will not be rectified except through that with which the first was rectified."[220]

What remains [to be said]: is that anyone who reads my article about unveiling and veiling cannot consider me to be against the education[221] of women as I am against their unveiling. That they would believe otherwise, is possibly based on the fact that the proponents of unveiling pretend they themselves hold a monopoly over supporting women's education as well. Every [religious or social] innovation in contradiction to Islam in this day and age is promoted in the name of science; even irreligion (*lādīniyya*) is expressed by its adherents as "secularism" [i.e., based on factual, scientific knowledge] (*ʿilmāniyya*),[222] seeking either to praise [irreligion] or hide it [from being attacked]! This expression, which confronts you throughout Egyptian newspapers, is often used to mean irreligion; [this is done] without any regard for [what true] science [entails], and showing no manners whatsoever for its religious readership [from any faith]. It [i.e. the use of the term 'secularism' instead of 'irreligion'] prevents [readers] from attributing to [the newspapers] the ignorance connoted by [irreligion], but it is no less than positively condescending [to believe] that they do not understand that the use of that word [secularism], at its core, is based upon irreligion [itself]!

---

[218] This was mentioned by 'Umar himself. al-Bukhārī notes 'Umar stating that, "My opinion coincided with that of my Lord in three things:...[secondly], the verse of veiling. I said, 'Oh messenger of Allāh, If only you commanded your women to veil, as both the righteous as well as the corrupt may speak to them, and so the verse of veiling was revealed..." See: *Ṣaḥīḥ al-Bukhārī* (402) Chapter: What has been said about the *Qibla*...

[219] Abū Bakr 'Abd Allāh b. Abī Quḥāfa (may Allāh be pleased with him), the first Caliph of Islam, who reigned from 632 to 634 AD.

[220] This quote is popularly attributed to Imām Mālik b. Anas, as opposed to Abū Bakr (may Allāh be pleased with them both). See: 'Iyāḍ b. Mūsa, Abū 'l-Faḍl. *al-Shifā*. Dubai: Jā'izat Dubai al-Dawliyya li 'l-Qur'ān al-Karīm, 2013, 591.

[221] For many, the term 'education' has become synonymous with the Western schooling system. Ṣabrī speaks at length here attempting to highlight that one should be wary of this latter form of education, as it often inculcates non-Muslim values within pupils, as opposed to purely informational learning, or education guided by Islamic values.

[222] In English, the word 'secularism' has no linguistic connection with the word 'knowledge'. However, in Arabic, as Ṣabrī points out, the word for secularism *ʿilmāniyya* is etymologically derived from the word for knowledge and science, *ʿilm*, as though implying that to fully apply knowledge and science at the political and social level is to implement a secular system.

Certainly, I do not forbid women from being educated, nor from gaining depth (*tabaḥḥur*) in the sciences for those who show great aptitude, however this on the condition that all this education and gaining depth happen in **schools specific to women,** that they do not mix with male students, and that their teachers are women like them.

If enough capable women cannot be found among them to teach the higher classes, male scholars should be given [temporary] mandate [to do so]; they could give lessons to their female students who would be covered in their *khimār*s. Naturally, I do not permit sending young girls to Western countries for them to study in their schools, and if it were the case that they absolutely must take these classes with the scholars of those countries, then recruiting a number of them to [teach in] our own lands and appointing them to [work in] our schools is safer than sending droves of our girls to their countries–to live there in a lifestyle similar to the daughters of the Europeans. **They would return years later, with no Islam left in them but the name, nor their nationality except the language,** and then, you would hear these Europeanized journalists hailing them with every kind of acclaim and flattery![223]

Amid all this intoxicating chaos (*ḍawḍāʾ al-mukhaddira*), Islam is lost. **How monumentally heedless are the parents who are thrilled and proud of those girls! What relaxation and comfort can there be for a sound nature, if someone were to replace his daughter with some other [unrecognisable] girl, even if the replacement is more 'knowledgeable' than the one replaced?!**

How is Prosperity Achieved?

The nation's renaissance[224] will not be found in the young daughters of its upper echelons attaining European doctorates in some sciences. Nor will it be found in their wealthy citizens having fancy cars through whose windowpanes they could see the world; their relationship with their fellow citizens being nothing more than to make their commutes

---

[223] Like praise and flattery directed by journalists at Ṣabrī's time to the Western-educated women of Stanley Bay.

[224] By "the nation's renaissance", Ṣabrī is referring to the popular concept of the Arab Renaissance (*nahḍa*), described in fn. 215. Unlike most Nahḍa thinkers, however, Ṣabrī advocates a rejection of imitating the social conventions of Europeans.

walking the streets more cumbersome as they fear colliding with these fast cars as they speed by.[225]

The world sees the state of Egyptian society; they see the men and women who board our public transport struggling to board and disembark, to even sit down, each trying to take more space than suffices him, leaving less for his neighbour. One man's foot tramples all about, and the cigarette smoke of another blows in his face, or he lets its ash fall on people's clothing; or perhaps you will see a woman next to you, holding a child, flies crowding the corners of his eyes, his lips stained with mucus or leftover food. Seeing this will make you regret boarding the tram car; [and yet] if you walk, the street cleaners will sweep dirt on you, [leaving you irritated all the same].

Compare the millions of Egyptian women, the likes of this child's mother, with the young Egyptian girls from the graduates of these higher Western schools, devoid of their veils, attached to Western women, and search in vain for the [truly] cultured Egyptian women lost between these two groups. A person cannot reside in Egypt without seeing people drowning from holding fast to their customs, even those which are reprehensible, as well as people obliterating themselves in reformation and Europeanization (*tafarnuj*).[226]

While writing these lines, I read the daily column of *Ustādh* al-Ṣāwī in *al-Ahrām*. [As one might expect,] he continues striving to the best of his ability to make free-mixing between young men and women widespread in Egypt, so that men may get to know and choose wives from among them. In support of this position of his, he published a letter sent to him by a certain Dr. Ṣ. N., who says that "he is very upset and annoyed by our Egyptian social system; he spent ten years between Germany, France and England, and only then truly saw the level of backwardness which plagues our families!"

And you, dear reader: you know from what we have highlighted previously, that amid the free-mixing, the getting to know one another, the [advanced] techniques [of flirting], and the roving of young men among the girls, seeking to examine and choose their options, they come to have no

---

[225] Automobiles were first introduced to Egypt as early as 1890, when Prince 'Azīz Ḥasan allegedly brought an English car to Alexandria, and certainly by 1901. By 1906, the khedival princes had established an exclusive automobile club, as vehicles became popular among Egypt's elite. Automobiles were often perceived as dangerous at this time, as cities were not laid out for cars, and there were few traffic regulations, leading to deadly incidents such as when an Italian driver killed an Egyptian and injured others in 1909. Nonetheless, automobiles became more widespread and would have been commonplace in Ṣabrī's Egypt of the 1930s. See: Volait, Mercedes, and Adam Mestyan. "Cars in Cairo." Academic Blog. *La Fabrique Du Caire Moderne - Duke University* (blog), September 27, 2020. Last Accessed: December 15th, 2023.
https://sites.duke.edu/cairemoderne/2020/09/27/cars-in-cairo

[226] Literally to "turn Frank", i.e. European.

need of marriage altogether.[227] The most objective testament to this is that the marriage crisis (*azmat al-zawāj*) is worse and the bachelors are more numerous in free-mixing countries than in the East.[228] Nevertheless, the *ustādh* columnist in question [al-Ṣāwī], continues issuing legal opinions and pontificating on issues of society, both secular and religious, despite lacking support from either transmitted [religious] or intellectual proofs.

The Ṭarbūsh[229] & The European Hat

I read two days ago in *al-Ahrām* an article by a writer on the margins decrying the persistence of the *ṭarbūsh* [i.e. fez] on Egyptians' heads.[230] He counts it as a social ill, a health hazard, an emblem of ignorance, and of being behind the times. In his eyes, it has no relation with Egyptian nationhood, except that the Turks enslaved them for a while and left a trace of that on their heads. The writer then decrees a legal opinion (*fatwā*) obligating the [Western] hat, the clothing of [modern] civilisation adopted today even by the Turks themselves, after they discarded the *ṭarbūsh*!

I sense in this complaint against 'Turkish slavery' a trace of English slavery, or an attraction to the present-day Turks in their modern dress by this Egyptian writer and his types, insofar as some Easterners, especially Muslims, did not want to wear the European hat until the heretical Turks adopted it for themselves, and so it became preferred by others as well. They

---

[227] "Because the young men who have tasted the sweetness of this cohabitation and become attached to it are not in need of marriage, and in front of them is diversity in their choice of cohabitation, and this life of free-mixing with young women makes precarious their trust in them, and it makes them wary of marriage..." See pg. 80.

[228] For more on the early 20th century Egyptian marriage crisis, see: Kholoussy (n. 39).

[229] A contemporary and friend of Ṣabrī, the Turkish scholar İskilipli Atıf Hoca composed a work in 1924 titled '*Frenk Mukallitliği ve Şapka* (The Hat and Imitation of the Europeans)' denouncing the European hat and urging Muslims to maintain their practice of wearing the *ṭarbūsh*. A year later, in 1925, the *Şapka Kanunu* (Hat Law) was passed by the Kemalists in Türkiye enforcing the prohibition of the *ṭarbūsh* and seeking to enforce European modernity among the Turks. This law was opposed by scholars such as İskilipli, Said Nursi, and others. People in droves began to revolt against the law, and many were executed as a result. İskilipli was also arrested for his work and the case was brought to trial where he maintained his views. The chief justice would question him about his rigidness, complaining that both the *ṭarbūsh* and the European hat were made of cloth (i.e., insisting that both were the same in essence). In reply, İskilipli mentioned that both the Turkish and British flags were also made out of cloth, however the former was distinctly Turkish while the latter foreign. He was originally sentenced to life in prison for violating the *Şapka Kanunu*, but would soon find himself facing the death penalty after Kemalists urged the court for more. He was executed by hanging on February 4th, 1926.

[230] The *ṭarbūsh* would similarly be banned in Egypt in 1958 by Gamāl 'Abd al-Nāṣir as part of modernization reforms for the country. This eventually led to its rapid decline in the country. It can only be found worn today in Egypt by students and graduates of Al-Azhar University, though it remains popular in other countries such as Morocco, and in the tourism industries across the Arab world.

threw aside the *ṭarbūsh* such that it has [now] become completely discarded. As for the statement of the writer who considers [the *ṭarbūsh*] to be enslavement, I sense him [becoming victim to] a new enslavement altogether, which even made him forget his national [Egyptian] duty to the *ṭarbūsh*, whose being a national dress was doubled through the collective effort of the "*Qirsh* Project" and the charity of its factories.[231]

In truth, there is nothing that more clearly indicates ignorance and being behind the times, than considering the *ṭarbūsh* to be an emblem of ignorance and being behind the times.

This [is the case], while wearing the Western hat is not permissible for Muslims, as I have properly clarified in an independent work.[232] And still, at the head of every Egyptian newspaper there are Muslim and Christian jurists who leave the official [Grand] Mufti feeling redundant!

The reason for the resumption of the debate in *al-Ahrām* over the *ṭarbūsh* and the Western hat was the rains that came one evening last week. It rained heavily, and some of the *ṭarābīsh* (*pl.* of *ṭarbūsh*) needed to be newly ironed. Now, it rarely rains in Egypt, and its cost for those who wear it is insignificant. It does not compare, even in its entirety [i.e. all its parts together], to the cost of the Western hat, especially their premium varieties. All this is despite the *ṭarbūsh*'s beautiful splendour in the eyes of Easterners, which is absent in the Western hat, and one need not sacrifice [money] for its required maintenance and ironing except rarely.

Honestly, I think [what happened is] that some of Egypt's extreme reformists tried on the Western hat, publicly or privately, and it made their faces look ugly, such that they remained content with their *ṭarābīsh*! [Compare this with] how much we hear of the agonies of the Turkish people and their yearning for their *ṭarābīsh*, if not for the swords that hang above their necks.

Everything connected with the East and Islam, from manners to etiquette to covering one's modesty, to the veils of women and the turbans of scholars; all of that came to be seen as something to throw away and change for the most trivial reasons. So, there is nothing preventing–as I have

---

[231] The *Jam'īyat al-Qirsh* ("Penny Society") was an Egyptian welfare project which some reformers established to protect the Egyptian identity, and that was by gathering modest donations that would start with one coin called the *qirsh*, and through that they established a factory for producing *ṭarābīsh* in Cairo in 1933, and that is so that they did not have to import it from foreign lands. See: Ṣabrī (n. 70), at 100 fn. 1., *Majallat al-Risāla*, vol. 2, p. 9, and *'Aṣr wa Rijāl*, vol. 1 p. 120.

[232] The title of this work [translated into Arabic] is *Ḥukm Lubs al-Qubba'at wa 'l-Burnayṭa* ("Ruling on the Wearing of the Cap and the Bowler Hat"). It was originally written by Ṣabrī in Ottoman Turkish. See: al-Qūsī (n. 27), at 271.

written in my comments on the column of the Liverpool University student–someone from writing in a newspaper, and analogizing [my response to that] with the statement of the margin columnist:

> "If truth be told, the persistence of Islam in Egypt is a remnant of the Turkish slavery that endured under the banner of the Ottoman state in the face of crusading [i.e. Western] nations, that remained submissive before this state's might for centuries, and gathered their command and partners in plotting against it and weakening it for centuries more. Islam survived all those long centuries relying on it [i.e., the Ottoman state]. It never occurred to any Christian nation to do missionary work in any Muslim nation, until, after a lot of beating around the bush, this state perished, and Türkiye apostatized from its religion. Then, the opponents of the religion of Islam from every corner of the world, from within and without, began to make progress,[233] until it came to a point where [Islam] was not respected in its land [Türkiye] or among its youth. And the Jews, who used to be stricken with humiliation and poverty, dared to establish a nation-state for themselves in the middle of the Arab lands; none but Allāh Himself knows how long the age of Islam will last after such ominous signs![234] So is it appropriate for the Egyptians, descendants of the honourable pharaohs–as mentioned by Hudā Hānim Sha'rāwī[235] in her address regarding the 'Renaissance of the Egyptian Woman', and the radio speech broadcasted a few days ago, which became the buzz of all of Egypt–[for them to continue as Muslims] after the Turks themselves

---

[233] Ṣabrī speaks about the relationship between the abandonment of the Islamic state and widespread apostasy as a result thereof in *al-Nakīr 'alā Munkirī al-Ni'ma min al-Dīn wa 'l-Khilāfat wa 'l-Umma* (Repudiation of Those that Reject the Blessings of Religion, the Caliphate, and the Global Muslim Community), written shortly before the fall of the Ottoman Caliphate. See: Ḥilmī (n. 12), at 140-146.

[234] Ṣabrī's book, and the quoted text would have been written in the period between the two World Wars, after the Balfour Declaration committed Britain to eventually release its League of Nations mandate over Palestine as an independent homeland for the Jewish people. The independence of Israel was declared in 1948, well after this book was written.

[235] Hudā Sha'rāwī was a famous early Egyptian feminist leader, and a close contact of Muḥammad 'Abduh and Sa'd Zaghlūl. She attended the conference for women's emancipation in Rome in 1923 and met with Mussolini, who hoped for the emancipation of women in Egypt. Upon her return to Egypt she publicly took off her veil, causing a stir in the country. She was the first Egyptian to publicly discard the veil, and would often go about uncovered. She is widely beloved by Western Middle East scholars. She advocated an extremely gradualist approach for liberalising Egyptian society. See: Baron, (n. 44) at 35.

abandoned Islam by the grace of their great reformer?![236] That they should cling to it while it remains the clearest sign of being behind the times?![237] In Egypt there are reformers who, even if they are unable to stand up and crush Islam and its symbols with their swords, are at least capable of doing so with their pens."

The Education Muslim Girls Need

We now return to the issue at hand:

I propose that education–for most girls–should be restricted to that which concerns them; to arranging their homes or raising their children and refining their character, upon the principles of health, organisation, and [home] economics.[238]

In summary, they should be cultivated to become ideal mothers and wives, instead of being [taught to be] equivalent to men in everything, for that is neither possible nor beneficial.

The Issue of Gender Equality

The claim of [women's] equality with men, per the phrase "a woman is capable of everything of which a man is capable," is cited by one of Egypt's famous female writers from Plato. [In fact,] she placed it next to the title of her article published in *al-Ahrām*, which reads:

> "There is no work in the system of the social order for which the woman is specifically qualified as a woman, or for which a man is specifically qualified as a man, because man and woman are equal in what they have been granted of blessings and abilities. For that

---

[236] i.e. Mustafa Kemal Atatürk, founder and first President of the Republic of Turkey, and avowed secularist. Under his rule, the institutions of the Ottoman Caliphate and Sultanate were legally abolished, along with many other measures aimed at limiting the scope of Islam in Turkish public life.

[237] [Muṣṭafā Ṣabrī]: Viewing the *ṭarbūsh* as the emblem of ignorance and being behind the times is an indication towards this view [i.e. seeing all of Islam as such].

[238] For more on the history of Muslim debates on female education, see: Wright, Brian Christopher. "Teaching Women to Write: Weaponizing Ḥadīth Against Colonialism." *Die Welt Des Islams* 62, no. 1 (June 7, 2021): 78–108.

> reason, the woman deserves to participate in all work that man partakes in, despite her being of a weaker body than him."[239]

This is an empty claim. I have written (with some exhaustion) refuting it in the article on polygamy.[240] [They cling to their arguments] despite the fact that Plato contradicts himself with his call for equality, recognizing that the woman is of weaker body than the man; is increased fortune in bodily strength not a blessing of nature (*fiṭra*) and [superior] ability? [They persist also] despite the fact that distinction by increased physical strength is the very root of worldly leadership; through it lands are conquered and certain nations rule over others. This alone should be sufficient for you in refuting the claim of equality.

It is for that reason that the poet says:

Indeed, Allāh has created men for wars,
And women to fiddle with the hems of their dresses[241]

Not to mention, if we were to affirm that woman can reach equality with man, and that she is capable of everything of which he is capable, she will not stop at the limit of equality, but will surpass him, because man is not capable of everything of which woman is capable. He is unable to carry a foetus in a womb, or to birth a child, breastfeed it, nurse it, love and serve it, and to have longing and gentleness with it, as a woman is able to nurse, love, serve, long for and deal gently with it. So the claim of equality for the woman,

---

[239] Plato does affirm that there is no work for which men are specifically better suited than women, but this does not mean he believes men and women to be equal. On the contrary, he believes men are better than women at everything, even activities in which bodily strength is of no advantage. In Book V of *The Republic* he writes: [Socrates:] "Do you know of anything that is practised by human beings in which the class of men doesn't excel that of women in all of these respects? Or shall we draw it out at length by speaking of weaving and the care of baked and boiled dishes—just those activities on which the reputation of the female sex is based and where its defeat is most ridiculous of all?" [Glaucon:] "As you say," he said, "it's true that the one class is quite dominated in virtually everything, so to speak, by the other. However, many women are better than many men in many things. But, as a whole, it is as you say." [Socrates:] "Therefore, my friend, there is no practice of a city's governors which belongs to woman because she's woman or to man because he's man; but the natures are scattered alike among both animals; and woman participates according to nature in all practices, and man in all, but in all of them woman is weaker than man." See: Plato. *The Republic of Plato*. Translated by Allan Bloom. Second edition. New York, NY: HarperCollins Publishers, 1991, 133f.

[240] See pgs. 53-55.

[241] This is a line of poetry written by 'Umar b. Abī Rabī'a (d. 712) in his *Dīwān*. What he means is that men (not merely males, but proper, masculine men) are made for acts of bravery, warfare and so on, while women are created in a state of constant panic and worry. See: Ibn Abī Rabī'a, 'Umar. *Dīwān 'Umar Ibn Abī Rabī'a*, 1st ed. Beirut, Lebanon: al-Maṭba'a al-Waṭaniyya, 1934, 233.

that ultimately ends with her surpassing the man, necessitates the opposite of what it intends. This is false, and through it, the claim's falsehood [i.e., of equality] is likewise highlighted.

I saw the female writer who quoted Plato's words in support of women's equality with men in her aforementioned article, shift from the claim of equality to the claim of female supremacy over men, when she said, "Our being distinguished by motherhood means we have been supplied a great distinction over man, and all the abilities, powers and dispensations that distinction entails. That goes along with our participation with men in all by which they are distinguished."[242]

Were we to concede the meaning of [what she says here,] that the equality between man and woman which people are still striving to establish is ultimately self-defeating, then the men who claim to be advocates of women should prepare all their might. Why? Because they have now been charged with a new obligation–to establish female *supremacy* over the man, even beyond her [previous] mere equality.

[Who knows:] perhaps it is her passing beyond equality with men to the level of progress and supremacy that [actually] grants the modern woman the right to increase her unveiling to double that of men, or even far beyond such that she now appears in clubs[243] and gatherings half-naked!!!

Women Beautifying Themselves for Men Indicates Their Need For & Dependency on Them in Life

If we return to the matter at hand,

Then this state [of affairs] by itself–

What I mean is: women's recent preoccupation with unveiling to men and their public display (*tabarruj*) ancient and modern, this preoccupation to which we turned our concerned attention in this article - and which is undoubtedly in search of status in men's eyes - clearly indicates their need for and dependency on men. Their laity and elites alike, whether

---

[242] Recent studies indicate an increased prevalence of anxiety, depression, overall dissatisfaction with life, and other mental and physical health issues in women when compared to men. The reasons for this can be varied, but researchers highlight that domestic work, when added to paid labour, increases the amount of work women are globally expected to handle when compared with men, leading to this distress. See: Miller, Claire Cain. "Why Unpaid Labor Is More Likely to Hurt Women's Mental Health than Men's." *The New York Times, September 30, 2022, sec. The Upshot.* Last Accessed: December 15th, 2023.
https://www.nytimes.com/2022/09/30/upshot/women-mental-health-labor.html

[243] The "club" (*nādī*) Ṣabrī mentions here is not a nightclub, but rather a particular sort of country club which became popular in 20th century Egypt. Membership fees sort people along class lines; the wealthy are members of the most exclusive *nādīs*, while the middle classes make do with what clubs they can afford. *Nādīs* typically have various sports facilities and cafes, providing something for the whole family.

of past or present, cannot do without it. Men have nothing analogous to it, despite the fact that [men's] physical need for [women] is not less than [women's] need for [men], if not even more.

So the [source of the] modern woman's preoccupation with unveiling to men is clear [to anyone]. The veiled woman of ancient times was also preoccupied with unveiling and beautification in front of the man for whom she was reserved, i.e. her husband. Even in a marriage where a woman pays a price to her husband during the marriage process, giving him a dowry (*dūṭa*),[244] contrary to Islamic marriage custom whereby the husband gives the wife her dowry (*mahr*), even in that marriage [in which she, not he, has paid the dowry,] she draws near to her husband and displays herself for him.[245] It has never happened in the history of the world that a man approaches, displaying himself to his wife, similarly to how the bride draws near to the groom, nor will this situation ever arise in the coming generations. For [the love of] self-display is found in this world with the woman alone, and it will perish when she perishes. No revolution that happens among the educated and cultivated classes of women, or sharing in all aspects of work with men, will replace this instinctive social order.

This preoccupation with modern unveiling and publicly displaying themselves to men, this deep-rooted need within them to be beautiful, blended with their very blood and souls... This [state of affairs] is the clearly observable reality which alone is sufficient in indicating that they have ultimately been created for men, more than anything [else] they may do independently, all while men in turn have been created to undertake their [various] occupations in life.

So where, in all of this, is there 'equality' with men, let alone women surpassing them?!

What is the statement of the philosopher Plato, or that of the aforementioned article's author, Zaynab al-Ḥakīm,[246] in comparison with the expressions of the Wise Qur'ān, "Do they attribute to Him those who are

---

[244] *Dūṭa* refers to wealth paid by the bride's family to the groom upon the marriage. Still commonly practiced in South Asia, this practice is referred to as *dahej* (or *jahez*).

[245] The Islamic conception is the opposite; the groom pays the *mahr* (dowry) for access to intimacy, while she beautifies herself as she receives something in return. In this opposite type of marriage arrangement, if the dowry was the real reason for beautification, as opposed to a woman's docile nature, one would see the men of that culture dressing up and preparing themselves to be plundered by their women–but this is entirely an inherent female trait.

[246] Zaynab al-Ḥakīm was an Egyptian feminist radio personality who went by this name, meaning "Zaynab the Wise".

brought up in fineries and are not commanding in disputes?" [*al-Zukhruf*: 18] and "And one of His signs is that He created for you spouses from among yourselves, so that you may find comfort in them." [*al-Rūm*: 21]

If all mankind, the jinn, and the demons of this day and age were to gather to delineate the woman's role in life in a way more articulate than these two verses, they would be unable to do so.

Furthermore, this position does not diminish what [women] deserve of the utmost respect. Says Allāh the Exalted, "We have commanded people to honour their parents. Their mothers bore them in hardship and delivered them in hardship. Their period of bearing and weaning is thirty months."[*al-Aḥqāf*: 15] And the Prophet (ﷺ) states: "Your mother, then your mother, then your mother, then your father."[247] And he also says: "Paradise lies beneath the feet of mothers."[248]

In these verses and narrations, there is an indication towards the fact that a woman's most noble description is as a mother, and it is through that that she is distinguished and promoted above men when the two sexes are compared. Through that, the void of her comparative deficiency to him is replenished completely, replacing the shortcoming with [true] favour and preference, rather than something associated with 'equality' achieved without him, such that would make her exceed [him], as the writer claims.

–Tam–

---

[247] This narration, related by Abū Hurayra (may Allāh be pleased with him), was in response to a question posed to the Prophet (ﷺ) about the one most deserving of good treatment. See: *Ṣaḥīḥ Muslim* (2548b) Chapter: Being Dutiful To One's Parents, And Which Of Them Is More Entitled To It.

[248] Though there is no authentic narration with this specific wording, one finds a similar narration related by Mu'āwiya b. Jahima al-Sulamī who mentions that his father questioned the Prophet (ﷺ) about partaking in [voluntary] jihād. In response, the Prophet (ﷺ) asked if he had a mother, and when he replied in the affirmative, he (ﷺ) mentioned, "Then stay with her, for Paradise is beneath her feet." See: *Sunan al-Nasā'ī* (3104) Chapter: Concession Allowing One Who Has a Mother To Stay Behind.

UNVEILING AND LIBERTINISM

When the great poet *al-Ustādh* Muḥammad Ḥasan al-Najmī (d. 1349/1940)[249] came to read these invaluable chapters in the newspaper "*al-Fatḥ*", his poetic fervour grew inflamed [and he composed] the following ode (*qaṣīda*):

A people drowning in immorality claimed that
Unveiling and free-mixing were paths to dignity

Lying at a time when facing obscenity had become
Competed for, and in which people found nobility

Is revealing the private parts a virtue such that they
Be broadcast by these youth embroiled in stupidity?

What is with them and the girl seduced by what
They say, releasing with it absolute sheer lunacy?

Her dignity appeared, vulnerable for those desiring
Propelling to it, even the clumsiest of the cowardly

The statement, upon utterance, became in her favour
Leaving no palm to prevent, no gate shut tightly

They despised marrying her, her market remaining
After they disgraced her, of no value and no utility

With what were they tasked in tearing away her veil
Drafting for it such speeches and composing formally?

Taking advantage of the weakness in our needs
And leniency more befitting than inflexibility

Have all our great difficulties become hems

[249] Muḥammad b. Ḥasan b. Shāhīn al-Najdī al-Miṣrī was an Islamic poet of the last century. For more on his biography, see: al-Bayyūmī, Muḥammad Rajab. *al-Nahḍat al-Islāmiyya fī Siyar A'lāmiha al-Mu'āṣirīn*. 1st ed. Vol. 2. 2 vols. Damascus–Beirut: Dār al-Qalam–al-Dār al-Shāmiyya, 1995, 2/535.

Dragged by unveiling of unrestrained totality?

Or have they lost the path and been deceived
By the shine of this new, tattering [ideology]?

***

Has this all encompassing trial tempted and lured our
Youth from whom restless fervour is hoped and likely?

An advice unpacked with all its hidden wonders:
To establish our spring all who would love and fancy

Never sharpen the ears of the welcoming
To the call of the owl beckoning inactivity

They did not intend through it any goodness though
Seeing the powerful tolerating, they resorted to flattery

Perhaps the strong merely erred in deed, but the weak
Went about in praise, speaking of it pompously

Save yourselves and your family disrepute for when you
Do not fear it–it would only attach itself to you tightly

Strive to deter the donkey every time it seethes
To the pleasures of permissiveness braying loudly

Civility lies not in seeing the spirit of modesty
At the hands of libertinism perishing daily

Desires propelling the girl at will so she wanders
Desiring and passionate for whom she wills leisurely

However, it is knowledge whose light ultimately guides
The West of the world, when the East deviates aimlessly

–al-Najmī

BIBLIOGRAPHY

Arabic References

'Abd al-Fattāḥ Imām, Imām. 1995-1996. *Aflāṭūn wa 'l-Mar'a*. Cairo: Maktaba Madbouly.

Āl-Borno, Muḥammad Ṣidqī. 1996. *al-Wajīz fī Īḍāḥ al-Fiqh al-Kulliyya*. Beirut, Lebanon: al-Mu'assasat al-Risāla al-'Ālamiyya.

ʿAqqād, ʿAbbās Maḥmūd al-. *Saʿd Zaghlūl: Ṣīra wa Taḥiyya*. Cairo, Egypt: Maṭbaʿ Ḥijāzī bi 'l-Qāhira, 1936.

'Asqalānī, Aḥmad Ibn Ḥajar al-. 1959-1960. *Fatḥ al-Bārī bi Sharḥ Ṣaḥīḥ al-Bukhārī*. Vol. 9. 13 vols. Beirut: Dār al-Ma'rifa.

Bayyūmī, Muḥammad R al-. 1995. *al-Nahḍat al-Islāmiyya fī Siyar A'lāmiha al-Mu'āṣirīn*. 1st ed. Vol. 2. 2 vols. Damascus - Beirut: Dār al-Qalam - al-Dār al-Shāmiyya.

Fahmī, Māhir Ḥasan. *Qāsim Amīn*. Cairo, Egypt: Wizārat al-Thaqāfa wa 'l-Irshād al-Qawmī, 1963.

Ibn Abī Rabī'a, 'Umar. 1934. *Dīwān 'Umar b. Abī Rabī'a*. 1st ed. Beirut, Lebanon: al-Maṭba'a al-Waṭaniyya.

Ibn Abī Yaʿlā, Muḥammad. *Ṭabaqāt al-Ḥanābila*. Edited by Muḥammad Ḥāmid al-Faqī. Vol. 1. Cairo, Egypt: Maṭbaʿa al-Sunna al-Muḥammadiyya, 1952.

Ibn 'Āshūr, Muḥammad al-Ṭāhir. 1984. *al-Taḥrīr wa 'l-Tanwīr*. Vol. 2. 30 vols. Tunis: al-Dār al-Tūnīsiyya li 'l-Nashr.

Ibn al-Jawzī, Yūsuf Sibṭ. 2013. *Mir'āt al-Zamān fī Tawārīkh al-A'yān*. Edited by Fādī al-Maghribī, Riḍwān Māmū, and Muḥammad M. Karīm al-Dīn. 1st ed. Vol. 14. 23 vols. Damascus, Syria: Dār al-Risāla al-'Ālamiyya.

Ibn Manẓūr, Muḥammad. 1993. *Lisān al-'Arab*. 3rd ed. Vol. 4. 10 vols. Beirut: Dār Ṣādir.

Imām, ʿAbd al-Fattāḥ. *Aflāṭūn Wa 'l-Mar'a*, n.d.

Jawziyya, Ibn al-Qayyim al-. 1994. *Zād al-Ma'ād fī Hadyi Khayr al-'Ibād*. 27th ed. Vol. 5. 5 vols. Beirut - Kuwait: Mu'assasat al-Risāla - Maktaba al-Manār al-Islāmiyya.

Kafawī, Ayyūb b. Mūsā al-. n.d. *al-Kulliyyāt Mu'jam fī Muṣṭalaḥāt wa 'l-Furūq al-Lughawiyya*. Edited by 'Adnān Darwīsh and Muḥammad al-Miṣrī. Beirut: Mu'assasat al-Risāla.

Kawtharī, Muḥammad Zāhid al-. n.d. *Maqālāt al-Kawtharī*. Cairo, Egypt: al-Maktaba al-Tawfīqiyya.

al-Mawsū'a al-Fiqhiyya al-Kuwaytiyya. 2006. 2nd ed. Vol. 37. 45 vols. Kuwait: Wizārat al-Awqāf wa 'l-Shu'ūn al-Islāmiyya - al-Kuwayt.

Munāwī, Muḥammad ʿAbd al-Ra'ūf al-. *Fayḍ al-Qadīr Sharḥ al-Jāmiʿ al-*

Saghīr. Vol. 6. 6 vols. Beirut, Lebanon: Dār al-Ma'rifa li 'l-Tibā'a wa 'l-Nashr, 1972.

Muqaddam, Muḥammad Aḥmad Ismā'īl al-. *'Awdat Al-Ḥijāb*. Vol. 10. Riyadh, Saudi Arabia: Dār al-Ṭayyiba, 2007.

Qurṭubī, Muḥammad al-. *al-Jāmi' li Aḥkām al-Qur'ān*. Vol. 2. 20 vols. Cairo, Egypt: Dār al-Kutub al-Miṣriyya, 1964.

Qūsī, Mufriḥ b. Sulaymān al-. *Al-Shaykh Muṣṭafā Ṣabrī Wa Mawqifuhū Min al-Fikr al-Wāfid*. Riyadh, Saudi Arabia: Markaz Malik Fayṣal li 'l-Buḥūth wa 'l-Dirāsāt al-Islāmiyya, 1997.

———. *Muṣṭafā Ṣabrī al-Mufakkir al-Islāmī wa 'l-'Ālim al-'Ālamī wa Shaykh al-Islām fī 'l-Dawlat al-'Uthmāniyya Sābiqan*. Damascus, Syria: Dār al-Qalam, 2006.

Rāghib al-Aṣfahānī, al-Ḥusayn al-. 1980. *al-Dharī'a ilā Makārim al-Sharī'a*. Beirut: Dār al-Kutub al-'Ilmiyya.

Rāzī, Muḥammad al-. 1999. *Mukhtār al-Ṣiḥāḥ*. Edited by Yūsuf a. Muḥammad. Beirut - Sidon: al-Maktaba al-'Aṣriyya - al-Dār al-Namūdhajiyya.

Riḍā, Muḥammad Rashīd. *Fatāwā al-Imām Muḥammad Rashīd Riḍā*. Edited by Ṣalāḥ al-Dīn al-Munajjid and Yūsuf Khūrī. Vol. 1. 6 vols. Beirut, Lebanon: Dār al-Kitāb al-Jadīd, 2005.

Ṣabrī, Muṣṭafā. *Qawlī Fī 'l-Mar'a*. Edited by Muḥammad Wā'il al-Ḥanbalī. Beirut, Lebanon: Dār al-Lubāb, 2019.

———. *Al-Nakīr 'Alā Munkirī 'l-Ni'ma Min al-Dīn Wa 'l-Khilāfat Wa 'l-Ummah*, n.d.

———. *Mawqif al-Bashar taḥta Sulṭān al-Qadar*. al-Maṭba'a 'l-Salafiyya, 1933.

———. *Mawqif al-'Aql wa 'l-'Ilm*. Beirut, Lebanon: Dār Iḥyā' al-Turāth al-'Arabī, 1981.

———. *Qawlī fī al-Mar'a wa Muqāranatuhu bi Aqwāl Muqallidat al-Gharb*. Beirut, Lebanon: Dār Ibn Ḥazm, 1935.

Sarakhsī, Muḥammad b. Aḥmad al-. 1989. *al-Mabsūṭ*. Vol. 2. 31 vols. Beirut, Lebanon: Maṭba'a al-Sa'āda - Dār al-Ma'rifa.

Ṣāwī, Aḥmad al-. 1934. *Mā Qalla wa Dalla*. Cairo, Egypt: Maṭba'a Dār al-Kutub al-Miṣriyya.

Shantamarī, al-A'lam al-, and Ṭarafa b. al-'Abd. 2000. *Dīwān Ṭarafa b. al-'Abd Sharḥ al-A'lam al-Shantamarī*. Edited by Dourrieh Al-Khatib and Luṭfī al-Ṣaqqāl. Lebanon: al-Mu'assasat al-'Arabiyya li 'l-Dirāsāt wa 'l-Nashr - Dār al-Thaqāfat wa 'l-Funūn.

Sharīf al-Raḍī, Muḥammad b. al-Ḥusayn al-. 1986. *Dīwān al-Sharīf al-Raḍī* (*vol. 2*). 1st ed. Vol. 2. 2 vols. Tehran, Iran: Manshūrāt Maṭba'a Wizārat al-Irshād al-Islāmī.

Shilaq, Aḥmad Zakariyyā al-. *Min al-nahḍa ilā al-istināra: fī tārīkh al-fikr al-Miṣrī al-ḥadīth*. First printing. Cairo, Egypt: Dār al-Karma, 2022.

Yaḥṣubī, 'Iyāḍ b. Mūsā al-. 2013. *al-Shifā bi Ta'rīf Ḥuqūq al-Muṣṭafā Ṣalla 'Llāhu 'Alayhi wa Sallam*. Edited by 'Abduh Koshek. Dubai: Jā'izat Dubai al-Dawliyya li 'l-Qur'ān al-Karīm.

Yūsuf, Muḥammad Khayr b. Ramaḍān. *Takmilat Mu'jam al-Mu'allifīn*. Vol. 1. Beirut, Lebanon: Dār Ibn Ḥazm, 1997.

Ziriklī, Khayr al-Dīn al-. 2002. *al-A'lām*. 15th ed. Vol. 3. 8 vols. Beirut, Lebanon: Dār al-'Ilm li 'l-Malāyīn.

English References

Ahram Online. "El-Sisi Moves on Banning Foreign Publications Offensive to Religion." News site. Ahram Online, January 14, 2015. https://english.ahram.org.eg/News/120255.aspx.

Artvinli, Fatih, Şahap Erkoç, and Fulya Kardeş. "Two Branches of the Same Tree: A Brief History of Turkish Neuropsychiatric Society (1914–2016)." *Noro Psikiyatr Ars* 54, no. 4 (2017): 364–71.

Atassi, Muhammad Ali. "The Veiling of the City." *Al Jadid* 16, no. 62 (2010). https://www.aljadid.com/content/veiling-city.

Badran, Margot. "The Feminist Vision in the Writings of Three Turn-of-the-Century Egyptian Women." *Bulletin* (*British Society for Middle Eastern Studies*) 15, no. 1/2 (1988): 11–20.

Baron, Beth. *Egypt as a Woman: Nationalism, Gender, and Politics*. Berkeley and Los Angeles, California: University of California Press, 2005.

Bein, Amit. "'Ulama and Political Activism in the Late Ottoman Empire: The Political Career of Şeyhülislâm Mustafa Sabri Efendi (1869–1954)." In *Guardians of Faith in Modern Times: 'Ulama' in the Middle East*, 105:67–90. Social, Economic and Political Studies of the Middle East and Asia. Leiden, The Netherlands: Brill, 2009.

Cook, Michael. *Commanding Right and Forbidding Wrong in Islamic Thought*. Cambridge, UK: Cambridge University Press, 2001.

Cuno, Kenneth M. *Modernizing Marriage: Family, Ideology and Law in Nineteenth- and Early Twentieth-Century Egypt*. First Edition. Gender and Globalization. Syracuse, N.Y.: Syracuse University Press, 2015.

European Network Against Racism. "Forgotten Women: The Impact of Islamophobia on Muslim Women." ENAR, 2016. https://www.enar-eu.org/wp-content/uploads/factsheet9-european_lr_1_.pdf.

Eurostat. "Are More Babies Born inside or Outside Marriage?" Statistical agency. *Eurostat* (blog), April 16, 2018. https://ec.europa.eu/eurostat/web/products-eurostat-news/-/ddn-20180416-1.

Gharad, Amin. "A Torch in the Ottoman Twilight: The Life and Struggles of Şeyhülislam Mustafa Sabri Efendi (1286–1374/1869–1954)." *Journal of Hanafi Studies* 1, no. 1 (2022): 131–43.

Ghoussoub, Mai. "Feminism—or the Eternal Masculine—in the Arab World." *New Left*, no. 161 (1987): 3–19.

Goldman, Wendy. *Women, the State, and Revolution: Soviet Family Policy and Social Life, 1917-1936*. Cambridge, UK: Cambridge University Press, 1993.

Green, Emma. "The Debate Over Muslim College Students Getting Secret Marriages." *The New Yorker*, September 9, 2022. https://www.newyorker.com/news/annals-of-education/the-debate-over-muslim-college-students-getting-secret-marriages.

Hammond, Andrew. *Late Ottoman Origins of Modern Islamic Thought: Turkish and Egyptian Thinkers on the Disruption of Islamic Knowledge*. Cambridge Studies in Islamic Civilization. Cambridge, UK: Cambridge University Press, 2023, 44.

Hassan, Mona. *Longing for the Lost Caliphate: A Transregional History*. Princeton, NJ: Princeton University Press, 2017.

Herrera, Linda. "'The Soul of a Nation': Abdallah Nadim and Education Reform in Egypt (1845-1896)." *Mediterranean Journal of Education Studies* 7, no. 1 (2002): 1–24.

Hughes, Luke. "The Gym-Timidation Report: Exploring Gender Experiences in the Gym." Blog. OriGym, November 17, 2021. https://origympersonaltrainercourses.co.uk/blog/the-gym-timidation-report-exploring-gender-experiences-in-the-gym.

Khan, Fareeha. "Traditionalist Approaches to Sharīʿah Reform: Mawlana Ashraf 'Ali Thānawi's Fatwa on Women's Right to Divorce." Doctoral thesis, University of Michigan, 2008,

Kholoussy, Hanan. *For Better, For Worse: The Marriage Crisis That Made Modern Egypt*. Stanford, California: Stanford University Press, 2010.

Macaulay, Thomas Babington. "Macaulay's Minute on Indian Education," February 2, 1835. National Archives of India. http://www.columbia.edu/itc/mealac/pritchett/00generallinks/macaulay/txt_minute_education_1835.html.

Miller, Claire Cain. "Why Unpaid Labor Is More Likely to Hurt Women's Mental Health Than Men's." News site. The New York Times, September 30, 2022. https://www.nytimes.com/2022/09/30/upshot/women-mental-health-labor.html.

Moosa, Ebrahim. *What Is a Madrasa?* Edinburgh: Edinburgh University Press, 2015.

Plato. *The Republic of Plato*. Translated by Allan Bloom. Second edition. New York, NY: HarperCollins Publishers, 1991.

Quadri, Junaid. *Transformations of Tradition: Islamic Law in Colonial Modernity*. Oxford, England: Oxford University Press, 2021.

Rabasa, Angela, Cheryl Benard, Lowell H. Schwartz, and Peter Sickle. *Building Moderate Muslim Networks*. Center for Middle East Public Policy. Arlington, Virginia: RAND Corporation, 2007. https://www.rand.org/content/dam/rand/pubs/monographs/2007/RAND_MG574.pdf.

Rahman, Fazlur. "The Impact of Modernity on Islam." *Islamic Studies* 5, no. 2 (1966): 113–28.

Reeves, Richard V. "Redshirt the Boys: Why Boys Should Start School a Year Later than Girls." *The Atlantic*, October 2022. https://www.theatlantic.com/magazine/archive/2022/10/boys-delayed-entry-school-start-redshirting/671238/.

Russell, Mona L. *Creating the New Egyptian Woman: Consumerism, Education, and National Identity, 1863–1922*. New York, NY: Palgrave Macmillan, 2004.

Stadiem, William. *Too Rich: The High Life and Tragic Death of King Farouk*. New York, NY: Carroll & Graf Publishers, 1991.

Statista Research Department. "Total Fertility Rate in Europe from 1950 to 2022." Statista, February 28, 2023. https://www.statista.com/statistics/1251565/total-fertility-rate-in-europe

Tasca, C, M Rapetti, MG Carta, and B Fadda. "Women and Hysteria in the History of Mental Health." *Clin Pract Epidemiol Ment Health* 8 (2012): 110–19.

Victor, Terry; Partridge, Eric; Dalzell, Tom (2006). *The new Partridge dictionary of slang and unconventional English*. New York: Routledge. p. 1752. ISBN 0-415-25937-1., "Calls Bachelors 'Simps.': 'Afraid to Take a Chance,' Says Woman Referring to Club". *The New York Times*. 14 May 1923.

Volait, Mercedes, and Adam Mestyan. "Cars in Cairo" Academic Blog. *La Fabrique Du Caire Moderne - Duke University* (blog), September 27, 2020. https://sites.duke.edu/cairemoderne/2020/09/27/cars-in-cairo

Wolfinger, Nicholas H. "Counterintuitive Trends in the Link Between Premarital Sex and Marital Stability." Blog. *Institute for Family Studies* (blog), June 6, 2016. https://ifstudies.org/blog/counterintuitive-trends-in-the-link-between-premarital-sex-and-marital-stability

Wright, Brian Christopher. "Teaching Women to Write: Weaponizing Ḥadīth Against Colonialism." *Die Welt Des Islams* 62, no. 1 (June 7, 2021): 78–108.

Other References

Albert-Sorel, André. *Lucie Delarue-Mardrus, sirène de l'Estuaire, née-native de Honfleur*. Honfleur, France: Éd. de la Lieutenance, 1999.

Gīlānī, Manāẓir Aḥsan. *Sawāniḥ-e Qāsmī*. Vol. 2. Deoband, India: Muḥammad Aslam Qasmī, 1975.

Hugo, Victor. "L'Avenir de l'Europe." In *Actes et Paroles*, Vol. III. Paris: J. Hetzel, 1880. https://www.atramenta.net/lire/oeuvre5715-chapitre-53.html.
Hugo, Victor. *Les Misérables*. New York, NY: Random House, 2000.
Ṣabrī, Muṣṭafā. *Dini Müceddidler*, n.d.
Şehabeddin Bey, Cenab. *Evrak-ı Eyyam*. Istanbul: Dar Sa'ādat–Qana'āt Matbaası, 1915.
Tarakçı, Celal. "Cenab Şahabeddin (1871–1934)." In *TDV İslâm Ansiklopedisi*, Vol. 7. Istanbul: TDV İslâm Araştırmaları Merkezi, 1993. https://islamansiklopedisi.org.tr/cenab-sahabeddin.

INDEX

ABOUT THE TRANSLATORS

Muzzammil Aḥmad al-Nadwī currently serves as an Imam at the East London Mosque in London, UK, and as an Advisor with the Islamic Council at the Muslim Research & Development Foundation (MRDF). A native of Bihar, India, he grew up in the United States where he started his Arabic and Islamic studies. He then graduated from Nadwatul Ulama, Lucknow in 2017 and Al-Azhar University, Cairo in 2021. He completed his MA in Islamic Law at SOAS, University of London in 2022, writing his dissertation on Islamic criminal jurisprudence. He is pursuing a PhD in Ḥanbali studies at KU Leuven, Belgium, and completing his MA dissertation in legal theory (*uṣūl al-fiqh*) at Al-Azhar. He has memorized the Qur'an and is traditionally licensed in the major works of various Islamic sciences. He also teaches at several institutions locally and online, while engaging in other research and translation projects.

Junayd–Ian–Greer is a professional Arabic translator and Canadian convert to Islam since 2017. He is a graduate of McGill University in Canada, and more recently of the American University in Cairo in Islamic studies, authoring a thesis on the works of *Shaykh al-Azhar* Ḥasan al-ʿAṭṭār (d. 1250/1835). He has studied the Islamic sciences traditionally since his conversion in Egypt, Morocco, and Northern Nigeria.

www.ingramcontent.com/pod-product-compliance
Lightning Source LLC
LaVergne TN
LVHW041224080426
835508LV00011B/1073